Lewis Malka is the owner and founder of Lewis
in fine diamond jewellery and engagement ring
approach to premium jewellery sets him head a
competition.

Lewis' rising status and passion for premium jewellery sets his profile and
designs apart in the fashion and jewellery industry. With an ever increasing
reputation and a high profile client base that expands across the world, this
year is set to be another great year for Lewis Malka.

————

When making big decisions (and buying an engagement ring is a really big
one) getting some sage advice is essential. I can recommend this guide to you
without reservation. Lewis is an author and jeweller with both gravitas and
experience you can trust.
Harry Levy, President, London Diamond Bourse

Lewis Malka is the man to go to for your engagement ring. If you're about to
propose... call him! He is a talented jeweller with unique designs and knows
all there is to know about diamonds. He listens to what you want and works
with you to create your dream ring. Thank you for all your help Lewis and
looking forward to keeping in touch...wedding rings next my friend!
Mark Rogers

Lewis has great flair, charm and creativity, as well as huge integrity.
A real diamond.
Lucia Silver

Lewis really is the engagement ring king! Not only can he produce amazing
diamond rings but his knowledge, experience and advice with all jewellery is
second to none. I'd highly recommend contacting Lewis if you're looking for
something sparkly at a price you can afford.
Joel Lassman

Lewis has a true gift with diamonds! He has made many spectacular pieces
for me over the years and I adore each and every one. Very proud to call
Lewis a dear friend.
Vanessa Staples

Published by Filament Publishing Ltd

16 Croydon Road,
Beddington, Croydon,
Surrey, CR0 4PA
United Kingdom.

www.filamentpublishing.com
+44 (0)208 688 2598

Second Edition: 2018
Printed by IngramSpark

ISBN 978-1-912256-76-1

www.lewismalka.com

To Joshua, Jessica and Amelie

You three make it all worthwhile

xxx

I'd like to thank:

Tim Dingle
There's no way this book would have been written without you

Alex Arenson
For brilliant creativity designing and laying out this book

Harry Levy
For his lovely foreword you're about to read

Caroline Chapple
For her wonderful style and ease in which she drew all the cartoons

Rhowena MacCuish
For having an amazing eye and taking wonderful images

Laura Rice
For all the times I've sent her proofs and all those amendments

Helen, **Karen** and **Sophie** my three lovable sisters
Without them all I probably wouldn't understand women as well as I do

And of course my parents **Ruth** and **Hanania**
For planting the seed and supporting me every step of the way

CONTENTS

FOREWORD

by Harry Levy
President, London Diamond Bourse

It is a great pleasure to write this foreword for such a well timed, thoughtful and excellent book as this. I have been President of the London Diamond Bourse since 2011 and have over fifty years in the diamond and gemstone industry. I have seen many trends over that time, but there is a consistent theme in the questions people ask when they are about to propose, "Where can I get the best advice, the best ring at the best price?".

My own career began after dabbling in the gemstone trade while doing a Masters in mathematics. A few years later I left the academic world and became fully engaged in the gemstone trade and founded my own company in London, Levy Gems. I have known Lewis for over fifteen years and I have seen his progress from young jeweller, to wise and dependable member of the London Diamond Bourse. So enthusiastic is he that I asked him to consider joining the board in 2008. He makes great pieces of jewellery and knows about diamonds and all other facets of the industry.

When making big decisions (and buying an engagement ring is a really big one) getting some sage advice is essential. I can recommend this guide to you without reservation. Lewis is an author with both gravitas and experience you can trust.

I hope you make the best choice and come and see what we all do in Hatton Garden. Good luck, do your research and enjoy the pleasure of buying a beautiful and eternal diamond ring.

INTRODUCTION

Let me paint you a picture.

I had a voicemail from a guy and it went like this:

"Hi Lewis, you don't know me but I know you and you also know my girlfriend Khara, I'm Mark. Please can you give me a call as we have something to discuss."

Well it's at a time like this that several scenarios run through your mind. When I phoned Mark back, he explained that he was looking for an engagement ring and that as his girlfriend had been ogling my Instagram images for months now, he felt that I was the right person to make her a ring.

In the next two weeks Mark and I met on three separate occasions. Mark wanted it to be a surprise and had an idea of what shape diamond Khara wanted. We had managed to whittle it down to 6 different diamonds and a couple of different ring styles. Mark's plan was to propose on a Friday night and he wanted me to come round to the house on Saturday.

Like clockwork I was ringing the doorbell at 1 o'clock Saturday lunchtime. Khara opened the door. The second she saw me she burst into tears as she realised why I was there. She kept saying,

"What's going on?" and "I've got no idea what's happening"

To Mark this was perfect. Everything was going as planned. As I walked through the front door I noticed there were rose petals at the bottom of the stairs. In the living room there were two glasses of champagne, some cake and the celebrations were well underway.

The next 15 minutes Khara spent coming to terms with what was going on. We sat and chatted about the proposal the night before. When Khara finally composed herself she wanted to know when she was going to get her ring.

She wanted to know if I had come to deliver it and wondered what it looked like. Mark had originally proposed with an inexpensive ring from a costume jewellery shop. This way he had a token piece when he got down on one knee.

He explained that I was here to show her a variety of diamonds and a selection of ring styles. The element of surprise was captured. The romantic aspect of designing and choosing her dream ring as a couple was underway. I had brought round a variety of different shape diamonds, it was up to Khara to decide which she preferred.

She took plenty of time learning and understanding the 4Cs (the characteristics from which we decide which diamond we want). She had managed to narrow it down to two diamonds; a brilliant cut round and an Asscher cut diamond. Each shape stone had it's own unique design which was chosen. The couple requested that they had the rest of the weekend to decide on which style was best suited for Khara now and forever.

As she was in two minds, I decided to post the photo of her wearing both rings on my social media platforms. I thought I'd get a crowd vote. Which shape would everyone think would suit Khara's hand the best. Well she didn't need the general public to tell her what her gut had already said, which was that the round brilliant cut was best suited for her hand and lifestyle. On Monday Mark phoned me and confirmed that Khara would love the brilliant cut round diamond as her engagement ring. We confirmed the style of the setting and a few days later the ring was made in my workshop. They both came up to my office late Friday afternoon to collect the ring. Naturally tears followed.

It's this scenario which is typical in my line of work and this is why I get up every day and go to work. Well for most people it's work. For me it's a passion.

This is why I do what I do and how I came up with my tag line,

Give her what she wants at a price you'll love!

KATIE PIPERS ENGAGEMENT AND WEDDING RING

To love someone deeply gives you strength. Being loved by someone deeply gives you courage.

At the back end of 2011 I had the pleasure of meeting Katie Piper at a charity event. She was giving a talk and raising awareness about her foundation. A few months after the event Katie got in touch and asked me to help her with some alterations and repairs to some pieces of jewellery she had.

It was a few years later that Katie got in touch with me. I received a DM from her which went like this. "Hi Lewis, how are you? I've just got engaged and I'm ring less. Would you like to make it for me"? Naturally I jumped at the chance. The ring was made just a few days later and ready in time for Christmas. Katie finally decided on a double halo style ring and with it a full diamond wedding ring.

I'm proud to count Katie as one of my friends and was privileged to attend her wedding in November 2015. The earlier quote is an extract from her order of service pamphlet. I do believe that this perfectly sums up her relationship with her husband. These are her rings and also a quote from Katie. Thank you Katie!

> *"I love my rings and Lewis was so hands on throughout the process. The fact that he's such a lovely guy made it even more special. Thank you."*

SO WHY DID I DECIDE TO WRITE THIS BOOK?

What qualifies me to write about picking the perfect engagement ring? Who am I and more importantly, where did I come from?

Well here's my story. I hope it excites you because after all, you are the reason I decided to write this.

One of the most common questions I get asked, other than, "Where did you get your good looks from?" is "Have you always wanted to be a jeweller?"

The short answer is no. I always wanted to be a fireman, but the fact is that I became a jeweller and how this happened was quite by chance.

Traditionally most jewellers in Hatton Garden, the jewellery centre of the UK and located in London, have been in the family for a few generations. Not so much anymore.

I was 16 years old when I was first introduced to the back end of the jewellery industry. A friend of my parents was a manufacturing jeweller. He wanted to know if I was interested in helping out for a few weeks. I was intrigued by the offer and accepted. I was fascinated by what I saw. The attention to detail and the intricate work involved was mesmerising. This was for me.

With the help and support of my parents I looked into starting a course in jewellery making. I found one that was starting immediately at Sir John Cass School of Arts. It was an apprenticeship course and they assisted in finding me work placement. I loved it. It was exhilarating and I wanted to learn everything I could. From soldering to sawing, from filing to buffing, from polishing to setting, and from casting to moulding. All my friends were doing A level exams and then off for a gap year. Not me. This was it.

In 1999 I took a gemmology course and passed. I learnt so much that all it did was fill me with a desire to learn more. Diamonds are one of those things that like most people I am fascinated by. The fact that something so small has such beauty and lustre to command such a high price is incredible.

In the year 2000 I founded and started on my own business and focused on creating bespoke pieces for private clients. The best way, and in my opinion the only way to do this is to create a network of people who can, and will, happily refer clients to me. I joined a networking organisation called BNI and have been a member since 2003.

I joined the London Diamond Bourse in 2005 and a few years later was invited onto the board, and to this day I proudly sit as a board member as part of an 11 person strong committee. The fact that I have a say in the future of the diamond industry and can make suggestions to improve and evolve it, is something which excites me and that I'm proud of.

2014 was a special year for me. Having spent years with clients discovering their genuine needs and desires when it comes to jewellery, I took this insight and used it to create my very first collection. I re-branded and changed my business name to Lewis Malka London. I launched in July 2014 with a collection of 13 distinct designs with a focus on refinement, ensuring the stone(s) remained a true focal point with the metal merely complimenting. Each piece is hand crafted and bespoke to each client.

I continue to champion a personal approach within the fine jewellery sector, offering one-to-one appointments for a bespoke experience where customers are able to impress their own individuality onto the outstanding design and incredible craftsmanship that I have become known for. I myself continue to hand craft all orders for a unique personal touch.

To coincide with the launch of my first Lewis Malka London collection, my company began working with an award winning PR agency to help create awareness around the brand and cement me as the go-to expert in fine diamond jewellery. Since this appointment I have become a regular contributor to the likes of the Daily Mail, The Mirror, OK!, MSN and Huffington Post. In addition, the debut collection has starred in a variety of titles, most notably within Harper's Bazaar as part of their top 30 engagement rings, alongside household brand names like Cartier and Tiffany. As a result of this investment in PR, Lewis Malka London has seen a huge increase in website hits, social media followers and direct calls regarding the brand.

In October of 2014 I was approached by Eva Longoria and Ricky Martin and asked if I wanted to get involved with their charity evening they were hosting here in London, The Global Gift Gala. I didn't hesitate and I donated a diamond necklace for the auction which Iveta Lukosiute wore on the night. There were lots of famous faces there and more than £500,000 was raised. You can read all about it in a blog I wrote.

This increase in press coverage and in turn, brand awareness put Lewis Malka London on the celebrity radar. As a result I became the exclusive jeweller to philanthropist Katie Piper, working with Katie and her fiancée to design and create her stunning engagement ring in December 2014 and to later go on to make their wedding rings.

June 2015 was another milestone for me. It was only eight months ago that I decided to put together my ready to wear collection of engagement rings and these are the pieces that were shortlisted for Bridal Collection of the Year at the UK Jewellery Awards. It's an annual trade-only event to recognise people in all sectors of my industry. The awards night was held at the famous Tower of London as a black tie event. It's the trade version of The Oscars and I'm very proud. Thank you to the people who nominated me. I didn't win on the night, however I was really proud to have been shortlisted. They picked me out from over 160 people who entered.

So as you can see, it's been a busy time for me, things are going from strength to strength. When I'm not at work either sourcing diamonds or in the workshop crafting some beautiful pieces of jewellery, I enjoy running marathons, going to the cinema and seeing the arts. I also seem to have quite a geeks obsession with James Bond! Well, we've all got something. So with that and my three kids, I'm pretty busy and very content in life. Recently my jewellery was seen on the red carpet at the Royal world première of the James bond movie Spectre. Something I'm very proud of. I'm looking forward to seeing what the future holds.

So that's me. Now let me share with you my objectives and desires about this book.

What I intend to do over the coming chapters is to give you an insight into the diamond industry. Not just an overview, but also an in depth look at how the jewellery market works. Specifically the engagement ring market.

With over 25 years experience I'm sure you will take some tips away to help you make some important decisions when it comes to buying that dream ring for your girlfriend. I intend to cover everything from the traditional 4Cs, proposal ideas, all the way through to insurance guidelines. I want you to be as educated and informed as you can. I want you to ask the right questions when you sit in front of the salesman. I want you to know your carats from your baguettes. All the information you will need to buy her dream ring at a price you'll love is right here.

Some of the most common questions are:

"What makes the perfect engagement ring?" and "How do I get the best engagement ring for my money?" The answer to those questions, and many more, will all be unveiled in this first-of-a-kind book.

CHAPTER 1

WHY DO WE BUY DIAMONDS?

Sir Donald Munger: Tell me, Commander, how far does your expertise extend into the field of diamonds?

James Bond: Well, hardest substance found in nature, they cut glass, suggest marriage, I suppose it replaced the dog as the girl's best friend. That's about it.

M: Refreshing to hear that there is one subject you're not an expert on!

This famous dialogue was taken from the 1971 James Bond film Diamonds Are Forever. I'm sure you've guessed by now that this has to be one of my favourite films. To me this sums up the allure of diamonds. It's what diamonds are about. Marilyn Monroe sung the song Diamonds Are A Girls Best Friend. And according to De Beers, who are arguably the World's largest diamond producers, we are all meant to spend three months salary on the perfect engagement ring.

Why? How did the diamond become the ultimate symbol of love? Why is it that every culture in modern civilisation traditionally uses a diamond ring to propose to their loved one?

In this chapter, I will give you my expert advice to help you pick the perfect engagement ring. I'm going to break it down into three sub chapters to make this a bit easier for you to follow and understand.

First I'd like to ask you a question. For love or money... why do we buy diamonds?

Have you ever wondered why there is no way to buy diamonds on the stock market? You can buy almost anything else – sugar, gold, orange juice, part of a football club – but you can't buy diamonds anywhere.

There is a reason. If you are thinking of buying a diamond, you have to examine it carefully. The first things you're assessing are the 4Cs: Cut, Carat, Clarity and Colour. Each of these is vital. Take clarity for example. The diamond's internal characteristics include features such as clouds, cavities, graining and laser lines to name a few. These are often known as 'inclusions'. Which inclusions a diamond has, and where, makes a big difference to the price. You should also consider the symmetry, fluorescence and proportions amongst other things. An impossible task without carefully viewing it in person.

People increasingly ask me about purchasing diamonds as an investment. Their first question is usually, "Will I get a better return than I do on cash in the bank?" The short answer is no. If you buy a significant diamond ring from any high street jeweller, it will probably take you 25-30 years to make your money back on it.

The only sensible way to purchase diamonds as an investment is to go to a reputable diamond trader. The same goes for buying an engagement ring. You want to go as close to wholesale as possible. We all know about the dangers of using past performance as a guide to the future, but the wholesale price of diamonds does generally increase year on year. This has been proven since records began in the 1970s. My advice is that it's probably better to spend your budget on one larger stone than two or three smaller ones. Go for a solitaire engagement ring over a trilogy style one. The larger a diamond, the rarer it is. As with most things, rarity makes for a better investment.

Coloured diamonds are rarer still and we have seen yellows, browns, greens and reds coming onto the market recently. One fact is that for every 250 tons of ground mined there is only 1 carat of jewellery grade diamonds unearthed. Another fact is that for every 10,000 carats of jewellery grade diamonds unearthed, only 1 carat is a fancy coloured diamond. Most of the time this is a yellow one. These will command an even higher price and should make a profit more quickly. Our records show that these have gone up in recent times by as much as 30%, year on year.

Pink and blue diamonds are the rarest of all. In November 2010, Laurence Graff bought a 24.78 carat rectangular pink diamond at auction for £29million. You probably won't be surprised to hear that this was the most amount of money ever paid for a diamond at the time. When he was asked why he paid so much, Mr Graff replied, "To reduce my tax bill this year". Diamonds can be almost magically beautiful, but investing in them remains a hard-headed decision.

Now it's obvious that you aren't buying your engagement ring as an investment so to speak. It's a given that the investment in this process is your girlfriend. You love her. You want to do the best you can to make sure you get this right. Naturally the pressure is on to get her the perfect ring.

For most of us it's the third largest purchase we are ever going to make behind a home and a car.

There are thousands of ways to screw it up but that will be heavily reduced, and hopefully eradicated altogether by following my advice in this book.

CHAPTER 2

ENGAGEMENT RING ADVICE FOR GUYS

If you liked it, then you shoulda put a ring on it.
—Beyonce.

Before we get started, I'm going to be honest with you. The best way to buy her an engagement ring she'll love is to let her pick it out herself. She'll wear this ring every day. It must feel good on her finger and it must suit her lifestyle. Sometimes it takes trying on many, many diamond shapes and setting styles to determine which ring is truly "best".

But you still want to go it alone, don't you? Perhaps because you are that old romantic guy we read about. Maybe you want to surprise her. Or because you don't want her to be involved with pricing and payment issues. That's fine! If you put some thought into it you can buy an engagement ring that she'll love almost as much as she loves you.

LET'S LOOK AT THE CONSIDERATIONS

Number 1: Pay Attention!

Paying attention to her jewellery likes and dislikes is the first big step towards finding her the perfect engagement ring:

What metal colour does she wear now?

Most women have a definite preference. If she loves white gold or platinum, don't even look at a diamond or other stone mounted in a yellow gold ring setting.

What style of jewellery does she wear now?

Is it contemporary looking with bold styling?

Does she prefer vintage or Art Deco period rings?

Would you say that the jewellery she wears is classic, resembling those timeless pieces that never go out of style?

The best indication of her tastes is the jewellery she wears all the time, not items she only wears occasionally, because it's the full-timers that she's most comfortable with.

Number 2: Has She Hinted at her Likes and Dislikes?

Has she ever mentioned her favourite jewellery styles or pointed out engagement rings when you're shopping together? If not, take her shopping. It isn't difficult to steer yourselves towards the jewellery shops. If you want to be subtle, say you're looking for a new watch, but be sure to pause at the engagement ring counters. Maybe she has a friend who recently became engaged.

Does she like her friend's engagement ring?

Why or why not?

Does she like diamonds?

Some women don't. Sapphires, emeralds and rubies are also popular gemstones that are often set into engagement rings for women who don't like to wear diamonds.

Number 3: What Looks Best on Her Hands?

An elongated diamond, such as a marquise or oval, can make short fingers look more sleek but be careful not to overdo the look or it could have the opposite effect.

Wide bands usually make fingers appear even shorter than they are, so think proportional:

Women with long fingers can easily wear bold ring styles.

A setting that's extremely delicate could get lost on large hands, over-emphasizing their size and making the ring look smaller.

Number 4: Choose the Right Shape and Setting

Round diamonds are the number one shape chosen by brides, but maybe not your bride. She might prefer an elongated marquise, oval or pear-shaped stone, or a square or emerald cut diamond. Fancier shapes, such as hearts, radiants or cushions are another option.

Do you think she'd like a solitaire diamond set alone in a band, or would she prefer a cluster of stones? Her current jewellery can give you clues about her preferences. The halo ring is popular as it gives the illusion the central diamond is larger than it really is.

Number 5: Consider her Lifestyle

How will the ring fit in with her lifestyle? Does she work in a profession where fussy jewellery would look out of place? Even if she doesn't, remember that a pointed gem with high prongs could snag clothing (and people) and is harder to keep clean. Save that type of ring for gifts that will be worn on special occasions, not every day.

Number 6: What's her Ring Size?

Does she have rings that she wears on her engagement finger? Maybe a friend or family member could get hold of one of them long enough for you to have it sized. Of course, you'll have to swear the messenger to secrecy. Consider this though, both of her hands are not the same size. If she wears a ring on "that" finger on the opposite hand, it won't necessarily be the same size. Don't let that worry you though. If your jeweller is like me, then he won't charge for a resize.

Number 7: Consider a Loose Diamond

If you think you know which shape she loves, buy a loose diamond to show her when you ask the big question. This is a trend that I started and promoted on my website. The idea is that you still have the element of surprise and now the two of you still have the romantic aspect of shopping together later for the perfect engagement ring design.

Insider Tip: Pay attention to the style and colour of her current jewellery. Take into consideration her lifestyle when picking the ring. Consider proposing with a loose diamond.

CHAPTER 3

DIAMONDS ARE FOREVER. A BRIEF HISTORY

A diamond is just a piece of coal that handled pressure extremely well. – Quote unknown.

The famous phrase "A Diamond is Forever" was first penned in 1947 by a young copywriter working for N. W. Ayer & Son, Frances Gerety. But is this really true? After all, what is a diamond? It's just a lump of coal, isn't it?

Well yes and no. Diamonds have gone on to become the most precious of all natural "stones" in the world. They have also become the ultimate symbol of love and betrothal. You know as a lady when you get a diamond ring it's a gesture of intent that your boyfriend wants to spend the rest of his life with you. Let's not forget either that it was only in the late 19th century that diamonds were properly discovered. Prior to this they only appeared in a few riverbeds in India and the jungles of Brazil. They amounted to only a few pounds in weight a year. Towards the end of that century however is when the boom happened. Huge diamond mines were discovered near Orange River in South Africa and miners came from all around the world to be part of the latest rush where diamonds were being scooped out by the ton. Suddenly the market was flooded.

It was the British who had been financing and organising the South African mines and they soon realised that their investment was in danger. After all, the entire diamond price relied solely on the fact that they were rare and scarce. The financiers were rightly worried that with new mines popping up, the value of their diamonds would be reduced as competitors offered the same goods at cheaper prices.

One day all the major investors held a meeting. The conclusion was that in order for the diamond mines to succeed they had to join together. They had to unite and become one. They had to merge their interests into a single entity and become powerful enough to control production and preserve the illusion that diamonds were scarce.

The creation became known as De Beers Consolidated Mines Ltd. As De Beers took control of all aspects of the world's diamonds, it assumed many forms in order to protect its investment and growth on the world stage. It is claimed that at its height, which was most of the twentieth century, it controlled more that 95% of the world's diamonds.

De Beers proved to be the most successful cartel in the chronicles of modern history. All other commodities such as gold, silver, wheat, copper and property fluctuated wildly in response to economic times and have gone up as well as down. Diamonds have, with a few exceptions, continued to advance upwards in price every year since the Great Depression of the 1930's. It got to a point in the late 1970's that even speculators began buying diamonds as security against inflation and recession.

So here we have a tiny crystal of carbon and De Beers have to introduce this to the world in such a way that the price will increase year on year. They had to find the best way create and market them so that people would never want to resell them. They needed to instil in us that diamonds are valuable and that we should never part with them. We all know what the end result was, however how they went about it was fascinating.

They decided to market diamonds as a token of wealth, power and romance. To achieve this they had to control the supply and the demand. The message had to be sent out to men and women. The message was that diamonds symbolise love and are an inseparable part of courtship and married life. To stabilise the market De Beers had to endow these stones with a sentiment that would prevent the public from ever reselling them. They had to create an illusion that diamonds were forever. And when they say "forever" they meant in the sense that they should never be sold.

Bloody brilliant. It's a genius idea that has seen the rise and rise of diamond prices over the decades. This is when the advertising and marketing campaign began. It was a campaign so powerful that it was to change the way diamonds were perceived forever.

The year was 1938 and Harry Oppenheimer was recommended by his bank to travel from Johannesburg in South Africa to New York City to meet with the then president of a leading advertising agency. Oppenheimer's bankers called a meeting as they were concerned about the declining price of diamonds which were affecting the market worldwide. In countries like England and France diamonds were still considered to be jewels for only the very wealthy, such as the Royal Family and aristocrats. In countries such as Austria, Italy, Spain and Germany the idea of giving a diamond ring had never really taken off. So all that seemed to remain was the United States as the only real market for De Beers. As a matter of fact, in 1938 three quarters of the cartels diamonds were sold as engagement rings in the United States. However, as it turned out most of these stones were smaller and of lower quality than the ones which were sold in Europe and had an average price of around £50-£60 a piece. With this in mind, Oppenheimer and the bankers believed that a well orchestrated advertising campaign could persuade Americans to buy more expensive diamonds. An introduction by the bankers to Gerold Lauck, president of N.W. Ayer, took place.

Oppenheimer suggested to Lauck that his agency set out a plan for creating a new image for diamonds among Americans. He assured Lauck that De Beers had not called any other agency and they had exclusive free range to come up with what they felt would best suit De Beers. If their proposals met with his father's approval, then N. W. Ayer would be the exclusive marketing and advertising agents in the United States. Oppenheimer was happy to underwrite all the costs necessary for the research of the campaign. Lauck accepted his offer there and then.

It's pretty interesting what sort of things you uncover when you start to dig deep and research things. Once N. W. Ayer really started to sink their teeth into the American diamond market they found that since the end of World War I in 1918, the total amount of diamonds sold in America that were measured in carats had declined by around 50%. At the same time though the quality of the diamonds measured in dollar value had declined almost by 100%. A memo that was circulated by Ayer concluded that the state of the diamond market was "the result of the economy, changes in social attitudes and the promotion of competitive luxuries". It was further deduced that since "young men buy over 90% of all engagement rings" it would be crucial to inspire them with the idea that diamonds are actually not only a great gift of love, but the only true gift of love. And of course with this comes the added phrase "the larger the diamond, the more you love her". Similarly though, women had to be educated to accept that diamonds really are the only true gesture of love and an integral part of any relationship.

The scene was set. The brief was delivered and now the hard work began. Since the plan was to romanticise diamonds, and this would require subtly altering the public's perception on the way men go about wooing a woman, N. W. Ayer strongly suggested exploiting the relatively new medium of using motion pictures.

Film stars, these were the new icons of the world. The way we all saw things happening on the big screen was the way to go. Everyone saw himself or herself as a Clark Gable or Marilyn Monroe. These icons would be given diamonds to use as the symbols of indestructible love. In addition the agency suggested offering diamonds to Hollywood's heroes to be used in photo shoots and publicity shots that would then be published worldwide. Movie stars turning up at premiers would be draped in De Beers diamonds and then sent to all the newspapers and magazines around the world.

This would reinforce the story between romance and diamonds. Fashion designers would talk on the radio about the "trends towards diamonds". The advertising company N. W. Ayer also planned to use the British Royal family to help increase the public's awareness of how beautiful owning a diamond can be. A memo said, "Since Great Britain has such an important interest in the diamond industry, the royal couple could be of tremendous assistance to this British industry by wearing diamonds rather than other jewels". A few years later, Queen Elizabeth went on a well publicised trip to several South African diamond mines, and she happily accepted a diamond from Oppenheimer.

By 1941 the advertising agency had reported to its client that it had already achieved impressive results. The sale of diamonds had increased some 55% in the US since 1938 and sales were increasing upwards. Another brainstorming session was pencilled in and it was noted at the meeting that its campaign had required "the conception of a new form of advertising. There was no brand name to be impressed on the public. There was simply an idea."

It further claimed that, "a new type of art was devised and a new colour, diamond blue, was created and used in these campaigns."

It wasn't until 1947 however, in its strategy plan that the advertising agency strongly emphasised, that they wanted a psychological approach. They stated "we are dealing with a problem in mass psychology. We seek to strengthen the tradition of the diamond engagement ring. To make it a psychological necessity, we must be capable of competing successfully at the retail level with utilities, goods and services". They had defined as their target audience "some 70 million people, 15 years and older whose opinion we hope to influence in support of our objectives". They were to arrange for lectures to visit high schools across the country and give talks revolving around the diamond engagement ring. They were to reach out to thousands of girls in their assemblies, classes and after school social activities. It really was a ruthless way to achieve their objectives. Let's not forget that back then people got engaged much younger than they do today. Not every household had a television.

A few months later the agency explained in a memo to De Beers that they had organised a weekly slot called "Hollywood Personalities". They were to provide all the leading publications across the United States with the descriptions of the diamonds worn by movie stars and focus on certain celebrities that week. They were to continue their efforts to encourage all the news agencies to market the celebrities wearing diamond rings as symbols of love.

By now they needed to come up with a slogan. One that they tried but failed at was "I wish I had what she has". Thank goodness for that. De Beers weren't too happy with this and asked them to try again. They needed something that can be related to by everyone. It didn't matter if you were the accountant in the city or the mechanic's wife. They wanted something that would express romance and timelessness. Late one evening a copywriter for N. W. Ayer came up with the caption 'A DIAMOND IS FOREVER®', which was scribbled on the bottom of a picture of two young lovers on honeymoon. Of course the irony is remarkable. After all you can in fact chip a diamond. You can discolour a diamond. A diamond can shatter. We can even incinerate a diamond to ash. However it was the concept of eternity which perfectly captured all the qualities that the advertising agency wanted to ascribe to a diamond. Within a year 'A DIAMOND IS FOREVER®' became the official motto of De Beers.

So there you have it. From that day to this, the slogan which has transformed the value of some small meaningless piece of carbon into arguably the most precious and valuable commodity in the world was born. However it didn't end there. The key to the success of the advertisers and De Beers was consistency. They knew they needed to keep diamonds associated with luxury and superiority if they were to maintain their public awareness campaign, not only in the States, but around the world too.

In America, which remained the most important market for most of De Beer's diamonds, N. W. Ayer recognized the need to create a new demand for diamonds among long-married couples. "Chocolates come, flowers come, furs come", but such momentary gifts fail to satisfy a woman's psychological craving for "a renewal of the romance", N. W. Ayer said in a report. An advertising campaign could instil the idea that the gift of a second diamond, in the later years of marriage, would be accepted as a sign of "ever-growing love". In 1962, N. W. Ayer asked for authorisation to "begin the long-term process of setting the diamond aside as the only appropriate gift for those later-in-life occasions where sentiment is to be expressed". De Beers immediately approved the campaign. This is when the diamond eternity ring was born, but that's a story for another time.

So what can we learn from this? Well to my mind a few things. Firstly, if Mr. Oppenheimer hadn't come along and decided, with a few other minds, to take control of the diamond market instead of leaving each site finder to fight for their own business, then would we still find diamonds as fascinating? I doubt they would be as expensive as they are. I doubt that we would use them as the only token for an engagement ring. Would they still be as demanding? Probably not. It makes you wonder though, what would we be using as an alternative to propose with?

A lesson to be had is that you can take an object, plant an idea about it in someone's head, repeat it often enough and they'll believe what they hear. Something to think about. I do hope you found that as interesting as I did.

CHAPTER 4

HIGH STREET VS BESPOKE (OR WHERE DO I BEGIN?)

I never hated a man enough to give him diamonds back.
– Zsa Zsa Gabor.

I want you to understand exactly what it is that you are looking to purchase. It is no good just saying an 'engagement ring'. You need to understand what type of engagement ring you are looking for. Explore all the avenues where you could possibly find information. At the end of this chapter you will understand that all the information you need is right here, in this book.

You may have already experienced information overload - there's a plethora of places you can source information from, for example the Internet, books, magazines, forums, family, friends, enemies and YouTube.

The secret is not just to ask questions, but to ask **better questions**. You must ask these questions so you are 'armed' and prepared for that all-important purchase.

Failure is not an option - Eugene Francis "Gene" Kranz (born August 17, 1933) is a retired NASA Flight Director and manager. Kranz served as a Flight Director, the successor to NASA founding Flight Director Chris Kraft during the Gemini and Apollo programs, and is best known for his role in directing the successful Mission Control team efforts to save the crew of Apollo 13, which later became the subject story of a major motion picture of the same name.

You have been with your sweetheart long enough to know that now is the time to commit. You want to get married. You want to show her how much you love her. You want to give her the perfect engagement ring. The article which is regarded as the ultimate symbol of your love. How's it going to work? Do you just walk into a High Street jeweller and ask to see the selection? Do you go online and look for the cheapest and biggest sparkler you can afford? Or do you go to the library and do your research? Well the short answer is always research.

One dilemma you'll face is do you go to an ordinary jewellery shop or do you make an appointment with a bespoke jeweller? There is a common misconception with buying a bespoke ring. A lot of people are under the impression that bespoke means expensive. In actual fact the definition of bespoke means:

You get exactly what you want at the price you want to pay.

You may find there are limited choices in terms of High Street jewellers. You might decide to buy online. Just because it's online and appears cheaper doesn't necessarily mean it is cheaper. You will need to know about the 4Cs and why it is that a bigger diamond can be cheaper than a smaller diamond. If a diamond is cheap then it's cheap for a reason… but *Caveat emptor...* a Latin term that means "let the buyer beware".

What does the typical High Street jeweller look like? I'm of course referring to the shop itself not the salesperson. A lot, if not all of High Street jewellery shops tend to fill their windows with off-the-peg, mass produced, pre-manufactured goods. These days a lot of mass produced goods are manufactured abroad, typically in the Far East and India. **[Insider Tip: It's definitely not something I would endorse.]**

I was recently sitting with a client. After going through the process of choosing her engagement ring she commented on how enjoyable this was compared to browsing in a shop. She added that she had never considered having a bespoke ring made as she thought it would be out of her price range. It was her friend that said she should Google bespoke jewellery. Their budget wasn't huge and I appreciate that it's relative for everyone. The couple spent £2900 on her ring and she got exactly what she wanted at a price they were willing to pay. They had done their research.

I'm of the belief that the only advantage a High Street jeweller has over a bespoke jeweller is that they have a ready to purchase collection of jewellery. The profit margin must be quite large in order to have that amount of stock and still maintain their overheads.

It's no secret where to find information, the trick is understanding what is worthwhile versus what is useless. You may see a ring that looks beautiful. In your eyes it's better than the one next to it. Is it actually better value for money? It's all about making better informed decisions.

CHAPTER 5

THERE ARE MORE QUESTIONS THAN ANSWERS

Pictures in my mind that will not show

There are more questions than answers

And the more I find out the less I know

Yeah, the more I find out the less I know...

–John Lester 'Johnny' Nash, Jr.

The moment has come. You've been procrastinating for months and asking yourself "Is it the right time?" You have been online and found that most websites are generic and give almost the same information. You believe that you are a semi-pro, if not full professional in understanding diamonds. It's time to go into a shop and put your knowledge to the test. There is nothing more exciting than having a client who has done some groundwork and has a notebook full of questions.

Typical topics which will be in the notebook will include:

- DIAMONDS
- RING DESIGN
- COSTS
- THE 4CS
- INSURANCE
- PROPOSAL IDEAS
- AESTHETICS
- CULTURAL BELIEFS
- WHITE GOLD OR PLATINUM?

Why do I need an engagement ring?

Well it's the right thing to do. It was a trend started a few centuries ago and now, certainly since the early 1920's, it's become standard practice. Most importantly though, it shows the rest of the world that the lady you love the most is spoken for.

Why do diamonds appear cheaper online?

The short answer is that diamonds are like fingerprints. All as individual as each other. We need to peel off another layer of the onion beyond the 4Cs to understand the pricing of a diamond. You need to see a diamond before you buy. If it seems to good to be true then it probably is.

Why does it need to be a diamond?

Quite simply it doesn't need to be a diamond. A lot of people use other precious stones such as rubies, emeralds and sapphires. Surrounding these stones with small diamonds not only enhances the colour of the gem, but also keeps your costs down considerably.

Who should I go to, a bespoke jeweller or a retail shop?

It depends on your circumstances. It is generally easier to go to a High Street shop as they have pre-made solutions ready to wear. However, the advantage of going to a bespoke jeweller is that you get exactly what you want at a price you'll love. If you are taking your time and doing research then the time factor has no bearing on this.

Who are the GIA?

The GIA, or Gemological Institute of America, are renowned as the most precise diamond grading laboratory in the world. All prices of diamonds around the world are based on the certification of the GIA laboratories.

What shape diamond best suits her finger?

Typically in this scenario a round diamond suits everyone and size is down to preference. If you are going for a fancy shape, you will get better value for money versus a round diamond. However what you need to remember here is the shape of her finger. If she has long slender fingers, then it's best to go for an elongated shape such as a marquise, oval or emerald cut diamond. If on the other hand she has short fingers, and I don't literally mean her other hand is shorter. Then perhaps a cushion, princess or Asscher cut diamond would suit her better.

What style of jewellery does she wear now?

Have a look at what she currently wears and be observant. See the style of jewellery she has, perhaps take some photos to take to your consultation and show the jeweller. That way they can point you in the right direction.

What is the most popular shape?

The round brilliant cut diamond is the most popular.

What is the most expensive shape?

As a result of the round brilliant cut being the most popular, this makes it the most expensive. A very good quality one carat round could cost you up to £9000 and comparatively the same quality in another shape can be as much as 20% less.

What happens with insuring my ring and how much should I insure it for?

The best deal you'll get is to have it placed on your home content policy so it's a good idea to contact your broker. As for how much, I would always put the valuation at around 15% more than I've charged you.

What is the Kimberley process?

The Kimberley Process (KP) is a joint government, industry and civil society initiative to stem the flow of conflict diamonds – rough diamonds used by rebel movements to finance wars against legitimate governments. As a result of this any ethical jeweller will only use conflict free diamonds.

What happens if she hates her engagement ring?

Well the largest part of the money spent on the engagement ring is for the central diamond. I'm basing this on you having a solitaire. So the cost of having the ring re-designed is minimal compared to the initial outlay for the diamond.

What sort of diamond should I be looking for?

It's important to fully understand the characteristics of a diamond and it's properties, namely the 4Cs. I tend to advise going for a diamond in the colour range of F-G and clarity of vs2/si1.

What are the 4Cs?

This is covered elsewhere in the book, however it's a good idea to ask the salesman to explain it so you can get an idea of their knowledge and see how confident you are in their explanation.

What am I better off going for size, colour or clarity?

Well this is very much a preferential and sometimes a cultural decision. Personally I think it's the colour that's spotted the first. If you can get a large stone with a great colour and not necessarily a great clarity, yet a clarity that's not too bad to the naked eye, then you are bang on the money.

What if I don't know her finger size, is this going to be a problem?

That's not a problem. A lot of people bring me a ring she wears on the same finger but on the opposite hand. This is great as an indication, but both hands aren't always the same size. I always offer a free ring resizing service.

What metal would I be better off with, platinum or white gold?

Well there's no such thing as natural white gold. Platinum is a naturally brighter metal and harder wearing. I would go with platinum.

What ring style is the most popular now, single stone or halo design?

It's very easy to fall into the trap of going with what's "popular". Go with what looks the nicest on the hand, what feels comfortable and what is the most practical.

What is the waiting time for a bespoke piece of jewellery?

The usual turnaround or the average turnaround should be around 2-4 weeks.

Where is the best place to buy an engagement ring?

It's always a great idea to shop around and it's something I suggest to my clients. Make sure the person you are dealing with is a member of the London Diamond Bourse and that the diamonds they sell are compliant with the Kimberly Process and have been ethically sourced.

What is the London Diamond Bourse?

The London Diamond Bourse (LDB) is the only live trading floor dealing diamonds in the UK. Situated in the heart of Hatton Garden, which is London's diamond district, it is the best place for jewellers to source their diamonds and one of the places I work. It's estimated that around 85% of the U.K.'s loose diamonds come through the London Diamond Bourse. I would recommend using a jeweller who is a member.

Where and what is Hatton Garden?

Hatton Garden is the epicentre centre of the London jewellery industry. Geographically located in the City of London by Holborn circus, postcode EC1N 8NX, you will find over 100 independent retail shops, as well as offices and workshops such as mine.

Where can I try on some sample rings?

My best advice is to pop into a few shops and take notes. Everyone will be more than happy to help you.

Where do your diamonds come from?

The truth is that we don't really know where our diamonds originate from. A lot of our business is done on trust and we can guarantee that the person we bought the stone from knows his sources and so on. This way we know that all the traders are compliant with the Kimberley Process. It's the only thing that is not on a diamond certificate.

There are so many companies who have certified diamonds from various organisations.

Which is the best I should look for?

If you ask any jeweller who is worth their salt which company they prefer to grade their diamonds, they will all reply GIA.

When is the best time to buy an engagement ring?

There are two answers to this question. The first being when you are ready. The second is when it feels right to you. There are times in the year such as Christmas and Valentine's Day when it may take longer to get your ring, especially if it's a bespoke piece, so take this into consideration.

How much should I spend on an engagement ring?

The proper answer is as much as you can afford. If you ask about and look online the average person will reply three months salary. The reason for this is that in the 1980's De Beers embarked on an aggressive marketing campaign suggesting we spend three months salary on our loved one. Just spend an amount you are comfortable with.

How should a wedding band sit with an engagement ring?

Ideally you want the wedding band to be flush with your engagement ring. If possible you want to avoid a curve or knick in the wedding ring. No matter how well it fits, the rings will always separate and never sit how you want them to. Have the engagement ring well made with the angles correct for your wedding ring to sit flush alongside it.

Why should I come to Lewis Malka London?

Lewis Malka London offers the best of both worlds. On the one hand they are members of the prestigious London Diamond Bourse, the UK's only live diamond trading floor. On the other hand your jewellery will be made exclusively in their workshop. No need to have the ring outsourced to a third party, thus saving you money.

How long does it take to alter the finger size?

The main bulk of the work is making the ring. Compared to this the re-sizing of your ring should only take a day or two. In some instances it can be done during a lunch hour.

CHAPTER 6

WHAT ARE THE 4CS?

Big girls need big diamonds.
– Elizabeth Taylor

Diamonds seem to cost the earth, pardon the pun. The first thing we need to do is understand what makes up the value of a diamond. We need to know what it is that makes them so valuable. We need to know how they are graded. You see without this understanding how will you know if you are overpaying? How will you know why the price of a particular graded diamond varies so much from place to place? Most importantly though, how will you know if you are getting value for money?

I looked through some figures for the Office for National Statistics and they show that the provisional number of marriages in England and Wales increased by 5.3% in 2014. Furthermore, after conducting my own survey with clients who have bought rings from me in 2014, I can confirm the average amount spent on an engagement ring from 2011-2014 inclusive is £2758. If I break this down further, then I know the amount spent by 25-29 year old males is an average of £2500. Yet the average spent by 33-39 year old males is £6834.

With this amount of money being spent, I can't emphasise enough how vital it is to know your diamond before you buy. The journey to understanding diamond grading and pricing begins here.

These are the 4Cs and the main characteristics that make up a diamond's value:

- COLOUR
- CLARITY
- CUT
- CARAT

Let's start with understanding how the diamond grading came about.

Just recently, the President of the London Diamond Bourse, Mr Harry Levy, gave an interview to the World Diamond Magazine. In it he recalls how grading came about. Now, being in the industry for coming on 25 years, I'm often asked why the grading of a diamond starts at the letter 'D' and not 'A'. I'm pleased to say that I give the same answer as Harry. Below is an extract from that article for you to enjoy.

"Gemological laboratories were first set up as places to identify gemstones of natural origin. These early laboratories were set up in most jewellery producing centres, but were run through other bodies. This was because there was little funding available so they needed subsidising, and most importantly they had to be commercially independent to prevent fraudulent results. In the UK a laboratory was set up in Hatton Garden, London, and run by the London Chamber of Commerce.

Research had to be done in developing the methods of detection, so the laboratories were run by people with a scientific background, and this led them to become educational institutions trying to teach traders (and anyone else that was interested) the basics and, later on, more advanced gemological knowledge. Identification, research and education were their most important aspects until the grading of diamonds became necessary.

Initially diamonds were not graded to determine their value but as a method of communication. Traders had developed local 'languages' using descriptive terms such as 'white', 'yellow tints', 'light PK' (pique), 'small inclusions' and so on. This worked in localities where traders were in daily contact with each other and could compare goods, thus allowing them to ascertain prices and so be able to trade. However, this only worked in closed communities — each locality developed its own terminology. The most common were descriptive terms, but others used localities where the diamonds were found.

One such system is the Scandinavian Diamond Nomenclature (Scan.D.N) which uses terms such as 'River', 'Wesselton', 'Crystal', 'Cape' and 'Yellow'. Once you are involved in international trading, a system that all can understand and use is needed. Around the early 1950s the GIA developed its colour-grading system, using letters to denote colour. This is achieved through a series of "master stones" where each stone is perceptibly different from the previous one. The GIA decided to name the top stone (the one showing no colour) "D" and then graded them down to "Z". The colour of a diamond is then determined by comparing it to the master stones.

If the colour falls between a G and H for example, it will be classed as G, although some systems would grade such a stone as H. There is no confusion as the master stones are also named to adjust for this apparent discrepancy. Thus in the second system just mentioned, the H master stone would be a G using the first system. These games have been played between laboratories for years to show that each is using an independent system from the others.

The letter 'D' was selected by the GIA as the highest colour grade as this was the failure grade in American school exams. At that time the top colour was referred to as either 'A', 'A++', 'A+++', 'Super A', or similar terms by the traders in the market. D was a colour that was never used, so the GIA used this as the top grade knowing that nobody else had used this letter — this was recounted to me by Richard Liddicoat.

The clarity grade was adopted by all, using the descriptive terms such as 'flawless', 'very very small inclusions' (VVS), 'small inclusions' (VS), 'slight inclusions' (SI) and so on. Exactly where and how the divisions occurred in the different systems is not exactly clear.

Having established a system to grade for colour and clarity, the carat weight was always a given and the cut was also listed as a descriptive term, and so the 4Cs as a means to determine the value of a stone became available."

On to the 4Cs now and let's take a more in depth look at each one. Knowing that buying an engagement ring is a significant purchase, it's crucial that we understand the 4Cs of diamond grading before deciding which stone to buy.

It wasn't all that long ago that diamonds themselves became universally accepted and used as tokens of love. After all, we've only been mining diamonds for around 100 years and it's only since the late 1940s that diamonds themselves were suggested as the main stone with which to propose. Before then people used all kinds of different gemstones as their centre piece and decorated them with perhaps very small diamonds around the edging. Thanks to a masterpiece of marketing and advertising by De Beers in 1947 where it was declared worldwide that "A diamond is forever", we now use them as the main focus point when getting engaged.

Have you ever tried to buy diamonds on the stock market? Well you can't. Have you noticed that you can buy anything else, but you can't buy diamonds? There is a reason for this and I'm going to share it with you.

You see it's estimated that there are around 16,000 different varieties of diamonds based on their shapes, sizes and characteristics, and it would be impossible to keep a live market on all of these. Plus the fact that a "vs2" on one diamond will look completely different from a "vs2" on another diamond, depending on where the inclusion is located. My first bit of advice is to not buy online, regardless of the price, but to view the diamond in person before buying. Nevertheless, let's not get ahead of ourselves, nobody is buying anything until we understand the basics of the 4Cs. So let's begin the education.

Colour

Colourless diamonds are traditionally considered the most desirable since they allow the most refraction of light (sparkle). Off white diamonds absorb light, inhibiting brilliance. To ensure that your jewellery is of the highest quality, it's a good idea to look through a variety of diamonds to eliminate those of lesser colour grades. My suggestion when picking a colour for your ring is that you go for a colour grade between F and H. It's so subjective though and the truth is you won't see the difference once you have your ring on as you will never have two stones next to each other to compare. Also the price difference can be considerable between colours. Make sure you can see the difference and don't just do what your friends have done. It's your stone to enjoy forever.

Clarity

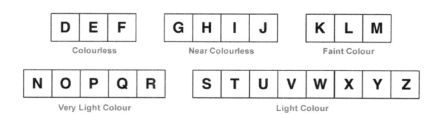

Most diamonds contain some inner flaws or inclusions that occur during the formation process. The visibility, number and size of these inclusions determine what is called the clarity of a diamond. Diamonds that are clear create more brilliance, and thus are more highly prized and priced. As a guide I would say that most people have inclusions in their diamonds, however it's the size of the inclusions that matter. Any diamond which is graded as "vs" shouldn't have any illusions that the naked eye can see. I recommend either a VS2 or SI1 as a starting point for good "eye clean" clarity.

Cut

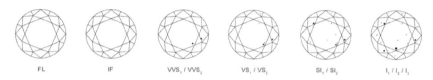

FL   IF   VVS$_1$ / VVS$_2$ VS$_1$ / VS$_2$ SI$_1$ / SI$_2$ I$_1$ / I$_2$ / I$_3$

This is probably the most important, and most challenging the '4Cs' to understand. In the first instance it can refer to the shape of the diamond you desire. This could be a pear, brilliant or emerald cut. However, the brilliance of a diamond depends heavily on its cut. You don't want a stone that's either too shallow or too deep. You need to ensure the proportions are correct and this is stated in the diamond report. You don't want anything lower than a grading of 'very good'.

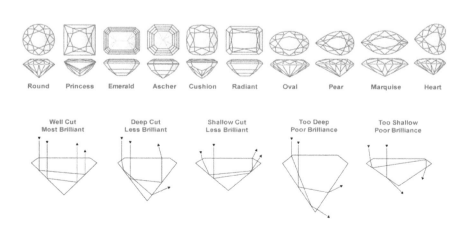

Round   Princess   Emerald   Ascher   Cushion   Radiant   Oval   Pear   Marquise   Heart

Well Cut
Most Brilliant

Deep Cut
Less Brilliant

Shallow Cut
Less Brilliant

Too Deep
Poor Brilliance

Too Shallow
Poor Brilliance

Carat

A carat is the unit of weight by which a diamond is measured. Because large diamonds are found less commonly than small diamonds, the price of a diamond rises per carat the bigger you go. That's to say that, for example, a one carat diamond could be £5,000 per carat, but the same quality two carat diamond will most certainly be more than £5,000 per carat. It's a curved graph the diamond prices are on. The bigger the stone, the rarer it is, the more expensive per carat the diamond is.

Images for ratios only
Not to scale

0.5ct   1.00ct   2.00ct   3.00ct   4.00ct   5.00ct

My advice is to always make sure you buy a diamond which is accompanied by a GIA report and from someone who is a member of the London Diamond Bourse.

Insider Tip: One thing to remember as well is that many "imperfect" diamonds can be perfectly lovely and make a very nice ring; jewellers are artists and can hide imperfections deftly under claws, or by placing them against backings that will shade certain areas of the diamond that are less perfect. Therefore you can still buy a diamond that will cost less but will still look absolutely lovely.

Harry Levy is among the diamonds, gem and jewellery industry's most treasured and veteran public servants.

He is, among others, President of the London Diamond Bourse; President of the Gemological Association of Great Britain and Chairman of the International Diamond Council.

CHAPTER 7

DIAMONDS DON'T ONLY COME IN WHITE

A kiss on the hand may be quite continental but diamonds are a girl's best friend. – from Gentlemen Prefer Blondes.

Diamonds are without question the most beautiful, precious and mesmerising objects in the world. Most of us are only aware that diamonds are clear, or white as referred to in the trade, in colour. Did you know that they don't only come in white?

PHOTO BY: LEIBISH & CO

Engagement rings are traditionally made with white diamonds. However if it's the wow factor you are after, why not opt for a coloured diamond in your engagement ring? Have something that screams out "look at me".

This doesn't mean that every diamond has to be a coloured one, but deciding to have a fancy colour in the centre and a white diamond on the shoulders will make your ring very attractive indeed.

Alternatively you may decide to have a white diamond in the centre and small pave diamonds on the shoulders which are natural pink in colour. They may not be as expensive as you think.

Famous diamonds like the Hope from India, the Yellow Tiffany from South Africa and the Williamson Fancy Pink inspire the imagination and are so valuable they seem almost like fictional objects of desire. Their size can leave you in awe and you can practically go blind from their beauty when in their presence.

Diamonds can also be a practical investment and there is nothing better than an investment you can wear. In markets where inflation rates have soared, investors have sought out diamonds as a way to put a hold on the value of their currency. The wealthy have used their diamonds to get them through tough economic times such as during WWII and the Asian economic crisis of 1997. And today there is no reason why we can't use fancy coloured diamonds

(FCD's) in our engagement ring.

The most popular of the FCD's is yellow and these range in colour, not like a white diamond from D-Z, but by its range of hue. Yellow is a diamond's second most common fancy colour. Yellow diamonds are sometimes marketed as "canary".

While this isn't a proper grading term, it's commonly used in the trade to describe fancy yellow diamonds. The terms to listen out for are 'fancy light', 'fancy', 'fancy intense' and 'fancy vivid'.

The style of the cut can also influence the colour. Cutters discovered that certain styles—typically mixed cuts like the radiant—can intensify yellow colour in diamonds that are toward the lower end of the D-to-Z colour-grading scale. When carefully fashioned as radiant cuts, many yellow-tinted stones—at one time called "cape" by the trade—can become fancy yellows when viewed face up. This perceived improvement in colour increases the price per carat. As an added benefit, the radiant style provides higher yield from the rough than a standard round brilliant cut.

CHAPTER 8

THE MAGIC HAPPENS HERE

I never worry about diets. The only carrots that concern me are the amount you get in a diamond. – Mae West

So you have picked a diamond and have taken onboard the 4Cs.

It's now time to witness the creation of a bespoke piece of jewellery. The engagement ring! Almost like the journey of Wild Atlantic Salmon, you will see the journey a diamond makes from the trading floor, to your treasured ring.

One of the most frequently asked questions is, "How long does it take to make an engagement ring?"

There is no simple answer. However you will see how a ring is made, assembled and finished in this short visual storyboard. One criticism that often falls upon people in my business is that everything is so secretive. I'm happy to open the doors and welcome you in.

The advantage clients have using me over one of my competitors is that I am the person who actually makes your ring. I still very much enjoy sitting in the workshop at the workbench and creating all these beautiful pieces that my clients order. Rest assured though, if it's not me making your ring but one of my team, I do have the last say in everything that leaves the workshop. Not any old ring is worthy of the Lewis Malka stamp.

During your initial consultation you will be presented with a selection of diamonds to suit your requirements. There will be some alternatives for you to peruse, giving you as much choice as possible and making sure you don't go over budget. This is where the fun begins. Unlike walking into a jewellery shop where everything is already made, you have the chance to create your own bespoke piece. You have the opportunity to hold each diamond and use the eyeglass.

You will see where the inclusions are in the diamonds. This unique experience gives you a way and understanding as to what makes these precious stones so valuable. Of course the bigger stone isn't always the most expensive. You will be shown each stone together with its certificate and an explanation as to what all the characteristics mean and how they affect the price of the diamond.

Once you have decided which diamond you have fallen in love with, then it's time to look at designs. Most clients have an idea of what they want, however, it's your opportunity to have your dream ring made and tailored to your desires. Just like no two diamonds are the same, no two rings are the same. You see even if two rings are identical in design and style, they will be different as the diamond sizes are different.

Now that you have decided on all aspects of the diamond and the ring design, it's time for some magic - and to conjure up your bespoke piece. The process of making your ring starts. Starting with the rough material, either as square wire or sheet metal. In this example the ring will be made in platinum. As we look through the process in these images you can see that all the skills come into play. There is soldering and sawing, cutting and hammering, setting and polishing. All these techniques and skills are required to make the perfect ring; your ring.

Similarly like the evolution of a butterfly, let's follow the evolution of your ring. Let us countdown this ten step process which will show your ring from workshop to finger.

10. The metal is formed for the band and the shoulders are cut out giving that distinct shape for the setting to fit into. You can see how intricate the process is by the fine saw blade.

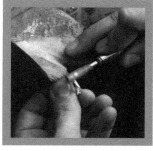

9. I'm defining the shoulders by sandpapering them with the help of my drill.

8. Time to make the setting now which is where the diamond will be set in.

7. Now the head and the shank are made, it is time to join the both of them together.

6. After filing the head and shank together so they are a perfect fit, it is time to solder them.

5. Now comes the filing. The objective here is to be rid of all the rough edges and further the desired shape.

4. Using a very fine drill bit, I'm able to clean up all the flashing and remove the surplus metal from the ring. This gives it a cleaner look and allows maximum light into the diamond.

3. The closer I get to the finished article the finer the tools are. This is a rubber wheel disc and it's gently tickling the head of the ring. I'm bright polishing the ring ahead of setting the diamond. The trick here is to not alter the main shape in the slightest but just to brighten the metals surface.

2. The diamond is now set in the ring whilst the ring is held in a clamp.

1. The final step in the process is to polish the ring ready for your loved one to wear.

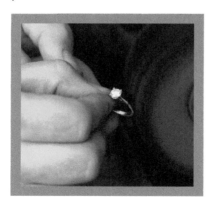

Zero. The diamond is set and the ring is made. Just giving it the once over before I contact the client to confirm collection.

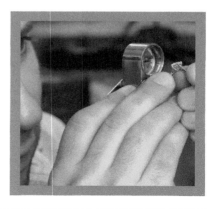

CHAPTER 9

THE PROPOSAL

You don't marry someone you can live with; you marry someone you can't live without. *−Unknown*

A proposal is such a special moment in any couples life as it is the start of the journey towards their future lives together. However, it is also very stressful, not only because you are worried about whether she will say YES, but also because there is so much to consider about the proposal itself.

To make things a little easier for you here is what you should consider before proposing, as well as some examples of the types of proposals that ladies (and guys) love, from the experts themselves, marriage proposal planning company, The Proposers.

How should I come up with my proposal idea?

Google is always a fantastic starting point for inspiration, as is Pinterest and Instagram. If this doesn't help, going to your nearest and dearest for advice is always beneficial as they are the people who know you and your partner the best.

Alternatively, you can seek professional help from a proposal planning company like us. Whether you just want help coming up with ideas, making sure that the proposal runs smoothly on the day, or the whole planning process, we can be involved as little or as much as you like, and the best part... you can take all the credit for it!

What sort of proposal should I have?

This is simple, you should tailor the proposal to your partner and it will be perfect.

If your partner loves red roses, make sure that they are present. If her favourite song is John Legend's, 'All of Me,' make sure it is playing in the background. You want the proposal to be about your relationship so why not print out photographs of the both of you together and hang them around your house, or create a timeline 'Love Story' of your relationship.

It's the little touches that might not seem like anything to you, which will make the proposal that much more special to her.

Should my proposal be public or private?

This, again, depends on your partner. If they are someone that would love a big, flashy public display of affection, then a huge show of your love in the middle of a public place will be the perfect proposal for them.

If, however, they are more reserved, a flash mob proposal in the centre of Trafalgar Square might not go down too well. You should do something more low-key and intimate instead!

Where should my proposal take place?

Before proposing you should make sure that the location is epic! The location will be part of your proposal story after all, plus you'll want a great backdrop for photos.

One of the most popular places to propose in London is The Shard. Why wouldn't it be? The view is incredible! Every city has it's own unique landmark or venue that would make the perfect location for your proposal. You just need to find it!

Alternatively, you can take your proposal across the seas to warmer, (and colder!) climates. Proposing on a beach at dusk as the waves crash beside you is always a good romantic idea. As is proposing under the Northern Lights.

So the big question now is how are you going to propose? Well here are twenty proposal ideas suitable for a range of personalities and budgets, which will help you decide.

Proposal One: Balloon Proposal

Take your girlfriend for a scenic walk where you will come across a beautifully wrapped gift with her name on. As she opens the gift a confetti filled balloon will float gently out of the box to reveal the words, 'Will You Marry Me?' As she is reading the balloon you will get down on one knee and ask her to marry you.

Proposal Two: Treasure Hunt Proposal

Do you and your partner have a favourite city, or places that you like to visit together? Organise a treasure hunt that will take you to these places. At each location arrange for your girlfriend to receive a gift, this can be flowers, chocolates, personalised photo frames, a singer performing your partners favourite song, or anything else that you think she may like. At the last stop on the hunt take the beautiful engagement ring out of your pocket, drop to your knees and ask, "Will you marry me?"

Proposal Three: Busker Proposal

Take a romantic evening stroll and as you are walking you will come across a busker who is performing your girlfriends favourite song. At the end of the song the musician will hand your partner a long stemmed rose with a tag that

says, 'I have a question to ask you...' This is when you get down on one knee and pop the question.

Proposal Four: Personalised Book Proposal

Personalised scrapbooks, photo books, or illustrated storybooks are a great way to propose, as you will have a keepsake to hold onto for the rest of your lives. You can use the book to highlight significant memories from your relationship, then at the end of the book include wording that says something along the lines of, 'But the best is yet to come...', which is when you will propose.

Proposal Five: Post-box Proposal

If your budget is on the low side, or you want to propose from the comfort of your own home why not do it by using one of our 'Post- box Proposals'.

These are a variety of unique proposals that can be sent straight to your door. From a movie night with personalised popcorn boxes and DVD cases, to wine and cheese tasting with personalised wine bottle labels we have a variety of proposals on offer. Visit www.theproposers.co.uk to find out more.

Proposal Six: Dress Up Proposal

A marriage proposal is an intimate moment in a couple's life. Therefore including those that are the most important to you only seems natural.

If you have a child or a pet you can include them in your proposal by dressing your pet up as Prince Charming and tying the ring around their neck with a cute bow.

Alternatively, if you have a child you can buy a t-shirt that says, 'Will you marry Daddy?" and there is nothing more adorable than that!

Proposal Seven: Christmas cracker Proposal

Christmas is the most popular time of year to propose so why not create a winter wonderland and spend the night enjoying a picnic hamper filled with hot chocolate, marshmallows and other sweet treats. You can also personalise a Christmas cracker so that when you crack it open the ring is inside.

Or, if you would like to propose on Christmas Day you can use the cracker idea when you are all sat down for dinner. This is great because it means that you can immediately celebrate with your family. Now that really is proposing with a bang.

Proposal Eight: Umbrella Proposal

If you live in England you will know that the weather is very temperamental so why not propose using umbrellas? This means that every time your partner sees one it will remind them of the day that they got engaged.

You'll need 15 people to help you with this and each will hold an umbrella with a single letter on it. This will eventually spell out 'Will You Marry Me?'

Ask your helpers to stand in a certain place, so that when you walk past with your girlfriend they can open their umbrellas to reveal the words. Your partner will be shocked when you get down on one knee and realise that it is all for her!

Photo © thelondonphotographer.eu

Proposal Nine: Boat Proposal

Arrange to spend the day out on a lovely canal or speedboat. As you are travelling towards a bridge, sipping on champagne and nibbling canapés your partner will look up and notice a banner saying, 'Will you marry me...?' Whilst she is reading the banner you will get down on one knee and pop the question.

Proposal Ten: Romantic Meal Proposal

Whether you hire a private dining room, or propose in the middle of a restaurant, proposing over dinner is always a fantastic way to pop the question. Depending on your budget you can plan anything from personalising a wine bottle label to say 'Marry Me', to filling the restaurant with secret singers to surprise your girlfriend by bursting into song. Anyway you do it we're sure you'll get a 'yes!'

Proposal Eleven: Iconic Landmark Proposal

No matter where you are in the world you will be able to find an iconic landmark to propose by or in. In London you can take your love to new heights by privately hiring out venues like Tower Bridge, The London Eye, or The Shard (to name a few). They all have fantastic views and make an incredibly romantic proposal setting.

Photo © Trillion Productions

Proposal Twelve: Room Decoration Proposal

You can create this at your house, in a hotel, in a privately hired room, in an iconic landmark, or even in an outside space. Ask someone you trust, whether it's a family member, friend or The Proposers, to come in and completely transform the room whilst you are out. Just imagine coming back to your room to see it filled with 5,000 rose petals, lines of candles and fairy lights strung everywhere. It's guaranteed to get you a YES!

Proposal Thirteen: Castle Proposal

Every girl wants to feel like a Princess, especially when they are being proposed to. And what better way to do that than by hiring a Castle (or Stately Home) exclusively for you both to enjoy. You can arrange to have a romantic candle lit dinner for two, then after dinner take a stroll around the grounds, only to discover that they have been charmingly decorated with fairy lights and candles. You can even go one step further and hire a musician to serenade you whilst you ask that all-important question.

Proposal Fourteen: Food Proposal

If your partner is a foodie using food is a unique and creative way to propose. You can spell out 'Will you marry me' using cupcakes, or even have a cake made into the shape of a ring box which you can put the ring into!

Photo © Berties Cupcakery

Proposal Fifteen: Fire words Proposal

Light up the sky with your love by proposing using fire words. This is great as you can do this in any outdoor space, (provided you have a permit), and just imagine your partners surprise when the words 'Marry me...' suddenly appear out of nowhere. It's sure to get you a YES.

Proposal Sixteen: Beach Proposal

A lot of people opt to propose whilst they are on holiday because the setting is so romantic. To keep the proposal a secret you can ask the hotel to help you arrange a candlelit meal for two on the beach where they can line the jetty with lanterns and rose petals, or to leave rose petals and champagne in your hotel room to surprise your partner with when you return. If you would like to take this one step further you can ask The Proposers to create a beautiful scrapbook full of memories that they will send to your hotel so your partner can receive it on the night as part of the proposal.

Proposal Seventeen:
Picnic Proposal

Have someone set up a picnic full of delicious cheeses, cakes, sandwiches and wine for you in a beautiful park or on top of hill so that you have a fantastic view. Suggest going for a walk with your partner where you will 'accidentally' come across the picnic. Your partner will be so shocked, and even more so when

Photo © Patrick Chatelain Photography

you pull out signs that you have made saying everything you love about your partner. The final sign will say, 'Marry Me...' and this is when you pull out the ring and propose.

Proposal Eighteen: Lip Dub Proposal

If your partner has a lot has a lot of close friends and family this one is perfect. Whilst you are enjoying a romantic stroll your partner's favourite song will begin to play. Suddenly you will join in by lip singing the words and dancing in time to the music. You will give each of her friends and family members a part, which they will perform one at a time in front of her as she is walking along. As the song ends you will get down on one knee and propose. Your partner will be so shocked, and as all of your friends and family are already with you, you can hold the engagement party on the same day!

Proposal Nineteen: Photo-bomb

Take your partner to their favourite spot, or a landmark and whilst there ask somebody to take a photo of the two of you. During the photo get two friends to hold up signs saying 'Marry Me' behind you. When you partner looks at the photo she'll be shocked to see that you've been photo-bombed. Whilst she is reading the signs it's your cue to get down on one knee and ask her to marry you.

Proposal Twenty: Flash mob Proposal

If you want to become a viral sensation over night, flash mob proposals are a brilliant way to do this. You can hire a group of singers to draw in a crowd by singing, or dancing in a public place. Then, when you have grabbed your partner's attention you can come out of the flash mob to propose. If you really want to shock them you can even take part by dancing in the flash mob!

These proposals are just some of the potential ideas you can create for your proposal. If you can't decide between them you can always take parts from different ideas to tailor the proposal to your relationship.

We have planned over 850 proposals in the last 4 years so you are in safe hands with us!

From dressing cats up as waiters and dogs as Disney characters to abseiling into caves to set up romantic dinners and hiring James Bond's speed boat we love a challenge and nothing is too much to ask!

If you would like any help planning your proposal, and would like to find out more about what we do visit: www.theproposers.co.uk.

Love
The Proposers
xox

Photo © Patrick Chatelain Photography

CHAPTER 10

MAKING SURE YOU GET VALUE FOR MONEY

True friends are like diamonds – bright, beautiful, valuable and always in style.
– Nicole Richie

It's one of those age old questions really and something that happens every day of the week. How can one not spend as much as one would like to, yet still get the same look and reaction from their engagement ring? Well it's not an easy question to answer. Here are a few tips and pointers to assist you when deciding what to buy from your jeweller.

To begin with, the most obvious thing is not to buy from a retailer. A retail shop commands huge overheads and when you consider that a jeweller isn't selling many rings a week, he needs to make a good profit to cover all his costs and these are factored in to the advertised price of the ring.

Here are some top tips based around the 4Cs. Let's start with the first C – "carat". This is the term related to the actual weight of the diamond. The way diamonds are priced is very interesting. There isn't a straight diagonal line from zero to infinity which we follow. Diamonds are priced on a concave upwards curved line starting from zero to infinity, and at certain carat weight breaks, the price increases. This is because the larger the diamond the rarer the stone and the more money per carat that stone commands. So perhaps you want a one carat diamond. This would have a millimetre spread of 6.4mm, now if you went for a 0.90ct diamond with a spread of 6.3mm then the price of the diamond will be considerably cheaper. Yet to the naked eye it will look like a one carat diamond.

The next C is for "cut" and this is referring to the shape of the diamond. I've already mentioned that the round brilliant cut is the most expensive cut.

Perhaps go for another fancy shape like the princess cut which will give just as much sparkle.

Now we come to the third C "colour" and this is a very funny one. The colour grade starts at the letter D and goes down to Z. The difference to the untrained naked eye between a D, E and F is nothing. The difference between an F and H is nothing too. So why pay all the extra money for a top colour diamond when the naked eye can't tell the difference between the two? It's not like she will be wearing both diamonds at the same time and see a comparable difference, is it? I would advise to get a H colour. Once you go lower you will visually start to see a tinge of yellow coming through, so perhaps avoid those ones. This is not to be confused with natural yellow diamonds.

This now leaves us with the last of the 4Cs that being "clarity". This is referring to how transparent the diamond is. Are there any inclusions that the naked eye can see? This is an interesting one and I encourage you to check when you do buy your diamond. I always pass over my eyeglass to my clients and point out where the inclusions are for them to see. With a VVS clarity diamond you will not see the inclusions with an eyeglass. With a VS clarity diamond you still may not see the inclusions with an eyeglass, this is dependant on where the inclusion is too, but generally to the untrained eye, you won't see it. Compare this with an SI clarity and you should be able to see the inclusions. They aren't necessarily black either. They could be white, black or even grey. So instead of going for a high clarity I suggest going for a lower grade and perhaps try to get one with the inclusion to the side that way it may be hidden by a claw.

These really are the considerations you need to think about when picking a diamond and trying to get value for money. The largest saving you will make will be dependant on understanding the 4Cs and putting the knowledge into practice. You could save thousands of pounds on these points alone. Don't be afraid to ask questions either. I always encourage questions from my clients and I teach them how to hold an eyeglass so they can see the inclusions, or not, for themselves.

Let me give you a few other quick pointers that can help you save a bit more money.

1. Stick to your budget. It's easy to get carried away, don't! Mention your budget to the jeweller and stick to it.

2. Instead of platinum choose 18-carat white gold. Both metals are just as strong as each other. And if your ring is priced up properly then you should save around £200.

3. Try to go to someone like me – a professional, by that I mean someone who can show you a selection of loose diamonds then pick the design. This will help as you don't have to take the limited selection they have in the shop and instead you can mix and match.

4. When designing or choosing your ring, make sure the band pinches in as it reaches the diamond. This gives the illusion the stone is larger than it actually is.

5. Opt for a smaller centre stone and have diamonds set on the shoulders. The small pave diamonds are very cheap compared to the difference between a 1.00ct and a 0.80ct diamond. So you still have a nice spread of sparkle to show off.

6. Perhaps have a rub over setting for your solitaire ring. This will give the illusion that your diamond is larger than it actually is.

7. Better still, reduce the centre stone slightly and opt for a popular halo design. This gives your ring a different dimension and increases the wow factor.

The fundamentals are in place and you know how to get proper value for money. Let's take a brief look at trying to get that Celebrity look for less. The way social media is today, we often see a celebrity's engagement ring as soon as his fiancé does. I get just as excited as you do to see these sparklers as there are many great designers out there and they often create some breathtaking pieces. It's not just the designs that make our jaw drop though, often it's the actual size of the diamond! With this in mind here are a few secrets for you so you can get the celebrity look for less.

The most obvious and first place to start would be to find the right supplier for you. There is a common misconception that if you find a jeweller to make you a bespoke piece, then that piece will be more expensive. Well this simply isn't true. The definition of bespoke simply means 'made to order' not 'let me overpay for that item'. So finding a bespoke jeweller such as myself simply means you will get what you want for the budget you decide. Have a look at their previous work and find out a bit about how they operate. See what trade organisations they belong to. You will be parting with a lot of money so do your research.

Onto the ring itself. Here are three examples, each of which I've had a look at and given a quote to the press about. Let's start with Phoebe Dahl. She has a fashionable and fun halo set engagement ring. Her centre diamond is around the 1.50 carat size, and with the diamonds surrounding it, it does look much larger. If you look closely at her band you will see there are three rows of smaller diamonds. The

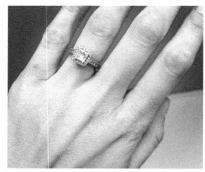

PHOTO: PHOEBE DAHL / INSTAGRAM

estimated value of this ring is around the £40,000 mark however a bespoke ring like this will cost from as little as £3,000. You should go for a cushion cut over a princess cut as it has a better spread to weight ratio. Meaning as there are no corners on a cushion cut diamond, there is no wasted diamond weight in the corners, therefore it will be a larger size. And instead of three rows of diamonds on the shoulders channel set like Phoebe's ring, just have one row of pave diamonds. It will look just as beautiful, if not prettier.

Next up in my selection of rings we have the remarkable diamond engagement ring belonging to X-Factor judge Cheryl Fernandez-Versini. When asked to comment on her ring, the one thing that really stood out was the absolute elegance and subtlety which this ring poses. There are a lot of flamboyant, larger than life, in your face celebrity engagement rings around,

but this is fantabulous! I think that if she just had her large 5.00 carat central diamond on its own, or in a halo setting, then it would have been very over the top. Yet adding two trapezium diamonds on the shoulders, which are faceted the same way as the emerald cut, just adds class to it. So how can we scale this down to make it more affordable? Quite simple actually. If we

PHOTO: CHERYL COLE/INSTAGRAM

THE ENGAGEMENT RING

were to start with a 0.50 carat central emerald cut and have a pair of baguettes on the shoulders weighing a total of 0.20 carats, then you should be able to pick up this ring from as little as £2,700. Perhaps even rotate the shoulder diamonds ninety degrees so we have a wider spread on the finger and voila!

The final ring belongs to Victoria Beckham. This would be the ring I would want to present to my fiancé. MSN UK asked me to give a comment on 10 of Victoria's rings and this is my favourite piece. You can see why.

This is the nicest piece Victoria has in her impressive collection. It is estimated the size of this almighty pear-shape diamond to be around the 15-carat mark and the clarity is probably eye perfect. My estimate would be along the lines of at least £1.5 million for this piece. Now you're wondering how you can get this look for a fraction of the price. Well the good news is you can. It does very much depend on your budget, but for around the £5,000 mark we can start to look at options. Firstly a pear shape diamond always looks larger than the actual weight of the diamond. As the diamond leads up to the point, it becomes shallower so therefore not as deep and not as heavy, which means a larger surface pro rata for the same as a round for example. With a lovely 0.75-carat plus diamond (colour and clarity dependant) there is no reason why you can't have a scaled down version of Victoria's ring sitting proudly on your finger.

The best advice though is to not pay retail! Come and see me, we will have a chat, it won't cost you anything. Then you can then make an educated decision on the ring. As always, I look forward to meeting you soon.

PHOTO: PINTEREST

CHAPTER 11

HOW TO GET THE PERFECT WEDDING RING

The three rings of marriage are the engagement ring, the wedding ring and the suffering. – Unknown

When couples that want an engagement ring made come over, we go through a process. The design aspect is something every lady wants to be involved with. The problems arise when people make an appointment for wedding rings and they haven't had the initial experience with me. The reason being that their engagement ring was made elsewhere. More often than not, the wedding ring is a plain, straight, band. The problem here is the fact that it doesn't fit nicely alongside her engagement ring. There might be a space between the two rings. The top of the wedding band is rubbing on the under setting of the engagement ring and causing a gap. The profiles don't match. The metals are different. The finger sizes are slightly out. The list goes on, however these are the main points.

The best time to make her wedding ring is at the same time as the engagement ring. This is not an expense you had in mind at the time, however, it can save you a few pounds later on. There is inevitably going to be some waste metal, in this case platinum, when making the engagement ring so if it can be incorporated into the wedding rings, it saves me buying a few extra grams at a later date. It might not sound a lot, but it could save you a few hundred pounds.

The fit and ultimate end look is very important to the bride to be. The focal point in her new relationship standing, needs to look it's best at all times, The future Mrs Bride will want the rings to look and sit perfectly. If you've gone for a solitaire ring, make sure the jeweller understands that you want a wedding band to fit close when it's all made. Ask to try on some wedding rings to see how the fit will be when your rings are ready.

The design of the engagement ring that seems to be on everyone's radar at the moment is the halo. It's a stunning piece and a great show. Two options are available to you here. You can either have a "fitted" wedding band so that the shape follows the outline of the ring or a straight band. If you go for the straight band, then from the top all you will see will be the engagement ring, this is how it should be.

One of the problems with having a fitted or shaped wedding band is that they always twist around on your finger. They rarely sit next to each other as you would like them too. There is a solution, and that would be to have the bands soldered together at the back once the wedding is over. The only drawback being that you won't be able to wear one without the other. Just another thing to consider.

One other consideration is should they have diamonds in their wedding band or not. Well this too is very dependant on their engagement ring. If they have a solitaire diamond which has a plain band, a plain band should sit alongside it, no wider than the engagement ring. If, on the other hand, you have diamonds on the shoulders of your wedding band then you should have the same stones on the wedding band and perhaps have them going all the way round. The reason for me suggesting they go all the way round is because the wedding ring is the same depth all over. This means that the ring will naturally spin around during the course of your day. With diamonds going all the way round, you won't have to stop and rearrange your rings each time you want to show them off.

One further point to contemplate is what metal to have your wedding ring in. On the face of it some people think that they've spent a lot of money on the engagement ring so don't need to worry about the wedding band. Well platinum is more expensive than white gold and they may appear to look identical, however, there is no such thing as natural white gold. When the gold is mined it is naturally yellow and then alloyed with palladium and then rhodium plated for the whiteness. Platinum is naturally white. However when they are next to each other and the rhodium wears off the white gold ring, or the high polish wears off the platinum ring, you will see a colour difference. The platinum is greyer and the white gold has a slight yellow tinge coming through. Together with the fact that platinum is more harder wearing than white gold and another problem arises. With the rings always sitting next to each other on the finger, the platinum one will, over time, wear down the gold one. It is always best to have both rings made in the same metal.

Once you have decided on the engagement and wedding ring's look and metal, it's time to consider whether or not you want engraving inside.

Some people think it's corny and some people get all squishy over it. A nice romantic way for the couple to have that private sentimental message and something unique, inscribed in their rings forever. It's not only words that can be engraved in a ring. You can have stones too. These are two prime examples of how you can have diamonds, sapphires or any stone you like, set inside your ring.

When the engagement ring was made, the client wanted me to hide a small diamond on the inside of the ring just to be quirky. There is engraving too, which sadly we can't see, which states "to the moon and back". The diamond here represents the stars you pass on the journey.

So whilst these are examples of rings that have engraving and stones set within, there is no reason at all why you can't have just a message, quote or date.

Some of the more memorable engraving to write inside wedding rings have been "Put me back on", "Don't be nosey" and "Why are you taking me off?"

Insider Tip: The best way to remember your wedding anniversary is to forget it, just once.

CHAPTER 12

INSURANCE AND VALUATION CERTIFICATES

I called an insurance company to get a quote. They gave me one of Oscar Wilde's best. – Jarod Kintz

Now you have decided to buy the ring, you need to ensure that your valuable ring is insured. Making sure that you're jewellery is fully insured can be a lengthy and expensive process. It's also something that only a handful of people bother to do. Granted it can be an expensive process, but the truth is it's all relative to everyone's standard of living. Typical costs for having an insurance valuation carried out can range from one to three percent of the total value of your articles.

Okay, but what is a valuation certificate? The short answer is, it's a certificate produced by an experienced jeweller with knowledge of fine metals and gemmology, who is able to provide an accurate replacement figure for your fine jewellery articles.

If you have a good insurance broker, and are with one of the big companies such as Chubb, Hiscox, AIG, or Sterling for example, then you will find that only articles valued at over £5000 per item typically, will need to be specified on your insurance policy thus listed on a valuation certificate.

However it doesn't end there. There are different types of valuations. Insurance retail replacement, manufacture replacement value, probate valuation, private sale valuation, and family division valuations for couples going through divorce.

More often than not in today's society, when you purchase a new piece of diamond jewellery, the retailer you purchased it from will provide you with a valuation certificate as part of the cost and service. Then all you need to do is pass it to your insurance company to make sure your new piece of diamond jewellery is put on risk, thus giving you peace of mind.

We live in a period now where we are finding more and more clients are coming in to have jewellery valued which has been bequest to them by a relative who has now passed on. These typically range from diamond engagement rings, diamond necklaces, diamond broaches, diamond earrings and even a diamond tiara at one point. A lot of these diamonds are old cuts and rose cuts which are not commonly found in today's retail store, and are from the 1920-1950's period. They are more likely to be found in antique markets and second hand jewellery shops, so getting the correct value can be a timely process.

There is a common misconception that diamonds are cheaper in different parts of the world such as South Africa or Canada. Well that's just not true. The bottom line is that diamonds are priced in dollars worldwide and then converted into the currency of the country you are living in. Once the stone is in the country, then the cost of manufacturing may be higher and with the profit, this makes the ring more expensive.

With that in mind, the replacement value of your article on a valuation certificate can and does change over the years due to the changes in the exchange rate, particularly the US Dollar to the Pound. Your insurance broker would recommend you have your certificate updated every 3-4 years. Please make sure you do it as values can change dramatically and you wouldn't want to be without the right money to be able to replace your sentimental piece of jewellery.

It's normally the same with new clients who have never purchased an expensive diamond piece before. A lot of research and due diligence has been done by the couple and they are parting with a substantial amount of money on a lovely diamond engagement ring. You've been through the process and the happy couple has chosen a lovely diamond for a solitaire ring. In this instance the diamond itself would have been assessed by the GIA (Gemological Institute of America). This normally prompts the question "why do I need a valuation certificate when I have this GIA diamond certificate?"

The GIA are an independent gem grading laboratory and as such they do not perform valuations. What they do is independently confirm the quality and all other characteristics that are used to determine a diamond's value.

What a valuation certificate does is qualify the value of that diamond at the current date on the certificate. The valuation will also take into account a replacement cost in the event of a loss or theft. The details as written out by the GIA are included in your valuation certificate. This will help the insurance company replace your diamond piece like for like in the event of them needing to replace your jewellery. This should also be accompanied by a photo of your piece in the valuation, which would avoid any confusion with the terminology used. So the short answer is yes, there is a difference between a diamond report and a valuation.

Here is another scenario for you to consider. In April 2015 the largest jewellery heist of the modern era took place. This is of course the robbery of the Hatton Garden Safe Deposit in the heart of London's jewellery quarter.

At the time the thieves got away with hundreds of millions of pounds worth of diamonds, gold and jewellery. This had jewellery-lovers asking themselves some serious questions. Is my jewellery adequately covered? Is my jewellery valuation up to date? When did I last have my specific articles checked out? Most importantly, what happens if my jewellery is taken into a jeweller and it gets stolen whilst in their possession?

The significant difference between this case and, say, the infamous Baker Street heist in 1971 is that this facility was, and is, mainly used by people in the trade: small businesses who make the pieces of jewellery you see in your high street jewellery shop window every day of the week. Hatton Garden, and its surrounds, is the most famous street in the UK for manufacturing jewellery, and it is here where lots of small independent traders work. Where the Baker Street deposit centre was pretty much all rented out by private clients, by contrast around 90% of the boxes rented out in the Hatton Garden area are rented out to people in the trade. These were independent diamond traders, stone dealers, diamond mounters, diamond setters, jewellery polishers, luxury watch traders and so on. There are so many facets to the industry (pardon the pun) that the effects and ramifications of this theft will last forever. For some people it unfortunately put them out of business - possibly a business that had been in the family for a few generations.

INSIDE TRACK

Let us say that you've had a bracelet, or a ring that was broken. Perhaps the diamond fell out the ring and needed replacing along with new claws. Perhaps the catch on your necklace was broken and in need of repair. What do you do? Well, assuming that you do not live in London you would be likely to take your piece to a local jeweller and he would then send it to a workshop in Hatton Garden. That jeweller, or jobber as they are known, would have lots of other jobs like this and probably get round to it in a week or two. During that time it would be held in the Safe Deposit Centre.

Imagine then that during that holding period the box was broken into and the piece - your piece - was stolen. You might not necessarily think that your piece has gone missing when you heard the news of the theft, but a day or two later you would get a call from your local jeweller explaining that this is in fact the case. First I suspect you would wonder how it got there in the first place when you only took your piece down the road to the local chap. Once he has explained, you would then start to ask yourself some questions, such as: Where do I stand? Was the piece insured and under whose insurance? Will I get it back? Will I be able to replace it like-for-like? So, suddenly the question posed earlier comes back into view: Is my insurance valuation up to date?

Let's imagine that I was sent a client's bracelet to repair by one of the small independent jewellers somewhere in the UK who I normally deal with. I give it out to the polisher to polish over night; he keeps it in the safe in the Safe Deposit Centre over the weekend and it gets stolen – who then is responsible? Who does the buck stop with?

First off, the insurance company would want to see your proof of ownership and then a receipt or a valuation certificate. Then they would ask for a receipt confirming that you gave it to the jeweller, and then a receipt, or proof that the jeweller posted it to me. After that they would want to see the paperwork between my polisher and me. Once they are satisfied that my polisher did have the piece, that it was a box that was broken into and that it was in fact stolen, they will want to see your valuation certificate. Now it will not be 100% clear how much cover the polisher has, and there will probably be a way for the client, yourself, to claim from your home insurance; however, the first port of call is with the polisher and his policy. Assuming he isn't covered, are you sure that you have the right level of cover in place?

So that old valuation that you had done over four years ago is not going to replace your piece, unless it was insured on a like-for-like basis. Speak to a jeweller and check your insurance policy without delay. Otherwise, it could be that your pieces go missing and you are left wondering if you're going to be able to replace them.

CHAPTER 13

WHEN SHOULD I GET ENGAGED?

I think men who have a pierced ear are better prepared for marriage. They've experienced pain and bought jewellery.
—Rita Rudner

According to a survey carried out by Chillisause, Christmas Eve is the most popular day of the year to propose.

Here is a list of the top 8 days of the year you might want to propose to your loved one on:

1. Christmas Eve
2. Valentine's Day
3. Christmas Day
4. New Year's Eve
5. Halloween
6. New Year's Day
7. Boxing Day
8. Your first date anniversary
9. Her birthday
10. His birthday

The survey found that almost a quarter of men will ask for their partner's hand in marriage on Christmas Eve, making it one of the most popular holidays for engagements. While many women may add a fairy tale marriage proposal to their holiday wish list, 22% of women would rather their men wait until Valentine's Day. The survey found that 20% of women want to get engaged on their anniversary, whereas 6% say a Halloween proposal would be sweet. So the difference between what women want and what they actually get seems quite split.

Christmas relationship statistics

Nearly 57% of men believe that you should be planning to spend Christmas together as soon as you start a relationship.

Women, on the other hand, are a little more cautious; nearly 51% of them believe it's okay to have different plans for Christmas until you've been together for at least a good few months.

Women's ideal proposal day	Men's ideal proposal day
• VALENTINE'S DAY	• CHRISTMAS EVE
• ANNIVERSARY OF THE DAY YOU MET	• VALENTINE'S DAY
• CHRISTMAS EVE	• ANNIVERSARY OF THE DAY YOU MET
• CHRISTMAS DAY	• HALLOWEEN
• NEW YEAR'S EVE	• CHRISTMAS DAY
• BOXING DAY	• NEW YEAR'S EVE
• NEW YEAR'S DAY	• NEWS YEAR'S DAY
• HIS BIRTHDAY	• BOXING DAY
• HER BIRTHDAY	• HIS BIRTHDAY
• HALLOWEEN	• HER BIRTHDAY

Only 10% of men and women think you should wait for a year or two.

Nearly 60% of men think you should plan to see in the first New Year with your new partner from the first few days of getting together; nearly 36% of women feel the same way.

Now that the pressure is on for men to formulate the perfect engagement this Christmas Eve, they might find comfort in knowing that 51 % of women want men to skip a theatrical speech and just ask straight out, "Will you marry me?"

How does that make you feel?

Does it put more pressure on you knowing roughly when you're expected to propose?

Or do you feel a bit more at ease because you know when it's possibly going to happen?

You have an end date in sight. You see looking at the statistics, it's very easy for society to dictate to you when you should propose to your girlfriend, when in truth the only person that knows when you should propose is you.

The biggest questions to ask yourself in this scenario are: Does this feel right?

Can I see myself waking up with the same woman for the rest of my life?

Most couples who come to me have been in a relationship for between two and four years. It is at this point that either independently the guy has decided that he wants to propose, or they jointly decided that this is the right time to get engaged. This brings up another hot topic for discussion:

Should a woman buy her own engagement ring?

This is a question that is very topical right now. Well, it always is when a guy is deliberating over the budget for the lady he loves.

Given how common it is for women to pick out their engagement rings, is it still taboo if they pay for them as well? This is something which has been going on silently for a number of years. Comments I hear first hand when couples are sitting together are,

"I'm happy to pay some extra for the larger diamond", and "If I'm paying too, then I want to have a say in the final piece".

Traditionally it's been ingrained in us for so long that men propose and they propose with a ring.

Today we are seeing more high-powered, highly paid women. In their eyes, they have ideals to live up to; for certain high-end ladies, it is paramount that their ring reflects their lifestyle.

Many people these days live together well before they decide to marry. They're sharing money, expenses and wedding costs. You could say that's partially the bride's money going towards her own engagement ring.

Statistics show that couples in the UK get married later in life than their parent's generation. The average age the man in the UK gets married at is 30.8 years and the average age to get married for women is 28.9 years. We are getting married older and these are the most recent figures from the office for National Statistics. As a result, many people who planned to wed this year have probably already lived together. On the face of it, day-to-day life may not change dramatically for those who have, nonetheless, it does bring about some significant changes and there is a lot to consider.

New Year's Eve

Yes it is one of the most popular nights of the year for a proposal. In fact, it can be as precise as clockwork, because as Big Ben strikes midnight, thousands of men will, to the surprise of thousands of girlfriends, get down on one knee and confess their emotions and ask for her hand in marriage. You thought romance was dead?

Failure to plan is planning to fail.

I had a panicked phone call from Mike one Wednesday morning. As usual he wanted to come in and look at an engagement ring. On the phone it became apparent that Mike wanted the ring that day, as his intention was to propose with it that weekend. Yes just two days later on their anniversary. A friend who had had her ring made by me earlier in the year recommended me. I told him to come at lunchtime. Mike came over and explained the reason why he had left it so late. He had actually forgotten that their anniversary was coming up and was reminded by his better half the night before. In a state of panic Mike had always intended to propose on their anniversary, but like most men, had forgotten when it was.

Mike had spent that morning looking in jewellery shops but couldn't find the "perfect ring" and wanted to have something made. We went through the process and I made Mike one promise. I told him that he would have his day and be able to propose with his desired ring that weekend. This is the reason I love what I do. Being the craftsman and diamantaire gives you such an advantage. It means that I know how long it takes to make a ring and can allocate my time accordingly. The solution for me was an easy one. Late home that night followed by an early morning. Mike came and collected the ring Friday morning before heading off for a romantic proposal weekend on their anniversary. Admittedly it's not the best way to work, but it's the relationship I want to build with my clients that is important to me.

The same sort of scenario happens with wedding rings. You may be surprised how many people leave these until the last minute too. All the planning that goes into the day could all be a waste of time. You can get the best venue, the best caterers and the most stunning dress. Yet if you don't have your wedding rings then you are going to run into all sorts of stresses on your big day.

Insider Tip: Have your wedding rings made at the same time as you have your engagement ring made. Not only will it save you stress on nearer the day, but it will also work out cheaper for you.

CHAPTER 14

WHERE IS HATTON GARDEN?

It's always best to start at the beginning and all you do is follow the yellow brick road Dorothy. – The Wizard Of OZ.

"Where is Hatton Garden?" or "What is Hatton Garden?"

I've heard that plenty of times over the years and it's still a surprise.

Perhaps it's because I've been walking the streets around here for over twenty-five years or maybe it's because I've just come to know it as my second home. It's like asking someone what Covent Garden is or even Camden Town.

They are synonymous for their own happenings and it's the same for Hatton Garden. The only difference is, that unless you are looking for an engagement ring or a piece of jewellery, you probably wouldn't have been to Hatton Garden. The Garden, as we who work there know it, is the jewellery centre of London. It's the only place in the UK which houses a live diamond trading floor, known as the London Diamond Bourse. Behind one of the nondescript building facades is my workshop.

At the time of writing this, there are over 87 different independent jewellery retailers at Hatton Garden. Eighty-seven! It's quite astonishing really and it can be quite overwhelming for first time visitors, and quite intimidating too. The only other comparison in my mind is the Diamond District in New York. These two are my favourite. They have the history. They have the allure. They have a certain type of mystique.

You may know what happens in London's famous Bond Street. It's a mix of high end designer fashion brands at the Oxford Street end of the road and as you get towards the middle and head down towards Piccadilly you will see shop after shop filled with large, bright, twinkly diamonds that only the fabulously wealthy people can afford. The likes of Cartier, De Beers and Asprey are well established and very much a part of the Bond Street historical architecture.

Just a couple of miles down the road, across town and towards Holborn, lies the historic London jewellery quarter that is Hatton Garden. There are three tiers of jewellery stores worldwide. There is the uber elite Bond Street equivalent. Then we have the small independents selling mid range diamond jewellery, some of which is bespoke, such as Hatton Garden. Lastly there are the multiples that appear on most High Streets. Those shops tend to run the lower end goods and knockout quantity over quality and it's all about turnover for them. As you turn into the garden from Holborn Circus, you will see these little jewels in the shop windows winking at you, beckoning you to come closer and see what's on offer. And running perpendicular to Hatton Garden we have Greville Street.

Hatton Garden takes its name from Sir Christopher Hatton, who acquired the land here from the bishops of Ely in the 1570s. The area surrounding Hatton Garden has been the centre of London's jewellery trade since medieval times. The old City of London had certain streets, or quarters, dedicated to types of business, and the area around Hatton Garden became a centre for jewellers and jewellery.

During the nineteenth century Johnson Matthey developed his gold and platinum business and the diamond trade expanded dramatically following the Kimberley diamond rush. Since the 1870's, the Hatton Garden area has established an international reputation as London's Jewellery Quarter.

During the Blitz lots of refugees fled popular diamond cutting cities, in particular Antwerp. They came to London and started to trade diamonds with the bullion merchants and traders in Hatton Garden. It was in 1940 that the London diamond Bourse was formed.

Near the top of Hatton Garden Street you can spot the plaque for Sir Hiram Maxim, who designed the machine gun and had workshops here.

So you've just got engaged.

You've now looked up or been told that Hatton Garden is "the" place to go to find your dream ring. However you get there and you choke. The occasion overwhelms you and you panic. What do you do and more importantly how do you decide who to go and see? Well it's all down to personal taste. The reason they all manage to do well is because from the outside they all look different. They all have different styles and they all have something very distinguishable about them. Just like we all have different styles and tastes. You might prefer a shop with a blue door whilst I prefer red. You may prefer a curved shop front whilst I prefer an arcade style frontage.

First walk up and down at least once without actually going into any of the shops and trying anything on. Just window shop. This will help calm your nerves and it will prevent the emotions and the moment getting the better of you. There is so much romance in Hatton Garden, it's difficult not to get carried away. Make notes of the shops you like and the ones you have seen a ring in that you may want to try on. Once done, go round again and this time go into these shops and ask the sales assistant if you can try on the rings you like. Just like most things in life, when buying something of this importance it's vital that you are happy and confident in not only the product, but also that there is trust in the person you are buying from. There is no harm in asking the sales assistant to give you a note of the ring you've tried on and then giving you twenty-four hours to make a decision. It's the nature of their business and a lot of people do that. Take your time and don't rush it. This is after all possibly the most expensive purchase you are going to make to date.

Aside from the independent retailers in The Garden, there are also people like me. All my pieces are made bespoke and without the overheads of a retailer. By working on an appointment-only basis you receive a very personal service. There was a gentleman who came to me with a scrapbook of images he'd printed off from the Internet, together with a list of about twenty questions he wanted answering before he would part with any money. The end result was that he, his wife, and his two daughters have now been clients of mine for the last eleven years and will continue to come back when the occasion dictates. I spent the time with him, earned his trust and I gave him the education which enabled him to make a knowledgeable and informed purchase. I love that about my clients.

This short overview of The Garden is a most fascinating place and not as intimidating as you might first come to expect. The occasion for heading down the famous street is a happy and exciting one. It's one which will remain in your memory forever. The journey you take in finding your perfect token of love will be told down the years with your ring remaining in the family forever. After all, we never really own a diamond we merely look after it for the next generation. Enjoy the moment!

CHAPTER 15

THE LONDON DIAMOND BOURSE

It takes only a few minutes to get married, but building a marriage takes a lifetime. A diamond is the final result of a long and intensive process – just like marriage. – Unknown.

The term bourse is Belgium and is derived from the exchanges that bring together brokers and dealers who buy and sell certain objects; in this case, diamonds.

The London Diamond Bourse first opened its doors in 1940. The necessity for London to open a trading floor came about mainly as a result of the occupation of Belgium in May 1940 by the Nazis. At the time Antwerp was the main diamond trading hub of the World, and had for most of its long history been the home of several active trade organisations. Amongst the refugees who managed to reach this country were a number of diamond merchants. In some cases they were able to bring their own stock with them. The fables go that the refugees managed to get their stock out by sewing the diamonds into the lining of their garments in order to smuggle their stock across the borders.

You would be forgiven for thinking that when the London Diamond Bourse was set up it was in a rather lavish old building in the heart of the City of London. Perhaps images of the Bank of England come to mind, not so. The setting for the diamond traders of its time, and the first location of the London Diamond Bourse

was established in Greville Street inside Mrs Cohen's Cafe, near its junction with Hatton Garden. A Committee and President were elected and, notwithstanding the very cramped and primitive conditions, the organisation worked with remarkable success.

From 1945 onwards there was an influx of members, some of whom were survivors of the Nazi occupation and concentration camps. As many of these had lost all their possessions and, in the cases of younger ones, missed their education, they started as diamond brokers with the help of those already established as dealers. In the mid 1950s the place was far too cramped and the London Diamond Bourse moved to the ground floor of 57 Hatton Garden as a temporary home. A few years later a new building was erected at 32 Hatton Garden, and with Barclays Bank on the ground floor, the London Diamond Bourse occupied the whole of the first floor.

For the first time the London Diamond Bourse had a worthy establishment, and in the years between 1960-1980 enjoyed prosperous trading. The membership grew to approximately 700. By the end of the 1980s even these premises proved too small, and when a new large building was planned at 100 Hatton Garden which would include space for many diamond offices, Barclays Bank on the ground floor and a safe deposit unit in the basement, a move was approved.

With changes worldwide within the Diamond Industry and various problems facing the UK Jewellery Trade during the 1980s, the diamond community found its numbers contracting. Many of the younger members had long felt that any valid reasons for the maintenance of two separate diamond trading organisations in London had fallen by the wayside. Pragmatism now lent force to their point of view. Negotiations with the London Diamond Club were accordingly undertaken, which were to lead to the Formation of the new united "London Diamond Bourse and Club".

This merger has been a very happy union for many years and continues to be so. However, at their AGM in 2014 it was decided to revert back to their original name of the London Diamond Bourse for many reasons including marketing and general logistics for business.

Today their membership is increasing. No longer are they such a xenophobic community. With the boom of social media in recent years, they have embraced this as a positive step towards assisting other facets in the industry. They are attracting members from all sides of the industry. No longer are members purely diamond traders, now there are members who are manufacturers, wholesalers and retailers to mention but a few. And as they go forward the aim is to increase our presence as the foremost diamond trading floor in Europe, perhaps even in the World.

I've been a member there since 2005. Not long after I joined I was invited to join the Board. This means attending monthly meetings and having a say in the future of the diamond industry as the older members retire and new challenges arise to entice younger members of the industry to join. I still sit on the Board as a proud member of the London Diamond Bourse.

Fact: It is estimated that around 85% of the UK's loose diamonds come through the trading floor of the Diamond Bourse.

The London Diamond Bourse (a member of the World Federation of Diamond Bourses) is an exclusive institution whose history, traditions and facilities make it unique in the UK. Members subscribe and are bound by a historic code of conduct which includes integrity, moral obligation, the highest standards of trade and best business practice. The London Diamond Bourse is recognised by the Foreign and Commonwealth office as a Trade Organisation and as such all their members are required to adhere to the Kimberley Process and provide annual certification to validate any trade in rough diamonds.

Being a member of their organisation provides my customers with assurance that they are trading with an individual who has pledged to uphold the traditions, principles of mutual trust and consideration within our industry.

Buying a stone or jewellery from a member of the London Diamond Bourse assures that the goods purchased are from a vetted professional of good standing who is accountable to the industry for their business dealings.

The London Diamond Bourse is the only Diamond Trading floor of its type in the UK. Membership to their organisation is earned, not automatically granted. As an organisation, their Board members are volunteers from their membership who do not receive payment or expenses for their work. Their sole purpose is to provide regulation and support to the UK diamond industry as well as inspire consumer confidence in the trade.

Fact: Any member who shakes hands on a transaction commits to it being a binding contract.

CHAPTER 16

SUMMARY OF YOUR JOURNEY

Success is a journey, not a destination. The doing is often more important than the outcome. – Arthur Ashe

As we reach the real beginning of your journey, it's time to recall the important factors and advice you've received to accomplish your objective.

The all-important yes!

It's all about asking the right questions and getting value for money. So let's go through it together and remember the most important questions to ask and factors to consider.

What are the 4Cs of diamond grading?

Refresh your memory and go over these so you know what to expect when you go to a shop. The easy two are the cut and carat. The cut is the shape you will go for and the carat is the size and this will be determined by your budget. The important 'Cs' are the colour and clarity. Picking an F si1 can save you a lot of money over a D vvs1.

Is the diamond certified by the GIA?

Make sure that your diamond has a certificate from the GIA. You want to know that your diamond has been graded to the highest level and the GIA are unquestionably recognised as the best worldwide.

Make sure you see the diamond in person and don't buy online. Yes there are lots of "bargains" online but remember if an offer seems too good to be true then it normally is. Take your time and make the effort to look at the diamond in person and make an informed decision. Two stones that are both graded vs2 will be different. One could have the inclusion in the top centre of the diamond and the other could be by the edge and round the underside. This can make a huge difference to the cost of the diamond.

Have confidence in her best friend

Find out what shape diamond she would prefer. Don't be afraid to confide in her best friend for a bit of advice. This will be one secret she won't tell her best friend.

Don't let fashion dictate the style of engagement ring. It's easy to get carried away with what's fashionable and lose sight of the end goal, your girlfriend's happiness. You may remember from an earlier chapter that around one in five ladies hate their engagement ring. Fashions come and go but this ring will last forever.

Where shall I go to buy my engagement ring, High Street or designer?

There is no harm in going to the High Street and trying on rings but do remember that they have huge overheads and will charge to compensate for that. Do some research and have a bespoke piece created. Remember my definition? Get exactly what you want at a price you want to pay.

How much should I spend on my engagement ring?

The short answer is as much as you can afford. Please don't break the bank and go into debt to buy this ring. You can always upgrade in a few years if you want something larger. You are about to start married life together and the last thing you want is financial debt from day one.

Those are some of the important questions you need to ask and inevitably they will lead to more. Go back through the chapters and refresh your memory. Some factors will be more relevant to you than others.

You should be able to sit with any jeweller, without being rushed, and understand all the answers you are given without an obligation to buy. If you start to feel the pressure then just make your apologies and leave.

Here are my top 6 tips to help you find your perfect engagement ring:

1. Stick to your budget and don't overspend no matter how tempting it might be.

2. Pick a diamond that is mid range on paper but looks high end on the finger. There is nothing wrong with a G/H colour and vs2/si1 clarity GIA graded stone.

3. Platinum is a better metal than white gold and it should only be around £150-£200 more expensive.

4. Picking a fancy shape (other than a round) will give you better value for money.

5. Make sure you have insurance cover in place when you collect your ring.

6. Try not to be persuaded by fashion and instead consider her lifestyle and taste.

CHAPTER 17

TALES FROM THE VAULTS

*Eat diamonds for breakfast
and shine all day!
—Unknown.*

Hopefully, you've got this far and realised that I love what I do. It's a good job: I've been doing it since I was sixteen and it would be a sad story – and a very different book – if I didn't enjoy coming in to work and helping to make people's dreams come true every day.

But you don't work in a job or an industry for as long as I have and not have some war stories to tell. And in Hatton Garden, of course, the stories tend to come thick and fast.

Naturally, everyone who's interested in this amazing corner of London inevitably asks about the obvious landmark moments in the colourful history of 'the Garden' – the estimated £200m burglary of the Hatton Garden Safe Deposit Company in 2015 (labelled by many as the largest burglary in English history), the Graff Diamonds robbery of 1993 and the immortalisation of the area in the Flanders & Swann song, *Down Below*. Even the road names have a rich and fascinating heritage.

But as jewellers, we tend to enjoy the personal stories of the people who work here a lot more than the headline-grabbing events that have occasionally put this wonderful part of our capital on the map for the wrong reasons.

Often, people ask me to tell them about the celebrities I meet in the course of my work or the most expensive piece of jewellery I've ever made. In the interests of full disclosure, you should know that when it comes to name-dropping, we're bit like doctors and priests: there's an unwritten – but no less unbreakable – agreement of client confidentiality.

For that reason, the names will remain a secret to protect the innocent (as well as those guilty of poor taste or behaviour). But here, for your entertainment, is a selection of stories from the vaults of my own life in Hatton Garden that have stuck with me over time.

The Premier League footballer and the enormous rock

This story involves a famous and, yes, unnamed WAG.

For those unfamiliar with the term (there surely can't be many of you out there) 'WAGs' is an acronym that refers to the 'wives and girlfriends' of top sportspeople, usually footballers. It was coined by the British tabloid press around the time of the 2006 World Cup finals when members of the England squad took their partners with them to the tournament.

The footballer in question came to see me because he wanted to buy an engagement ring for his girlfriend and, as many guys do, he chose a solitaire. At the time, one of the reasons he gave for buying the particular ring he did was so that his fiancée could have it altered if she wanted to.

He clearly knew her well, because alter it she did. And then she did it again. And again. And again. In fact, she increased it to such a size and proportion that it was just ridiculous – a crazy size.

I mean, I'm always pleased and grateful to be asked to do work for people, don't get me wrong; but it gets to a point where you just think, this is too much – enough is enough.

I don't mind at all if someone wants to make a change to a ring because it doesn't feel right. As I always say, the intention is that this is a ring that's going to be worn forever, so it needs to be right, and one of the issues when the girl hasn't chosen the ring is that it almost certainly won't be one hundred per cent perfect. But you do get to the point where you think that the changes being made are enough to affect the sensibilities of the person wearing it, never mind anyone else.

I knew the ring wasn't going to be practical for everyday use and she's such a petite girl with small hands that it just looked silly. But that was what she wanted.

The other thing that I remember about that particular purchase was sitting down with the player right at the start. He was picking out rings and there was one he was particularly interested in. I said to him, "You know, I'm not sure I'm happy about selling this stone to you."

He seemed quite shocked and asked why, and I told him it was because traditionally the man was supposed to spend three months' salary on the engagement ring. Now this lad was a top Premiership footballer, earning tens of thousands of pounds a week, so three months' salary would have added up to somewhere north of half a million quid and I thought it was quite a funny joke.

It would be crude to reveal here what he did eventually spend, but it was a pretty penny. He didn't like the joke, though. He plays abroad now, so I don't know if they're still together.

I did see the lady in question again in Bond Street not long after he proposed, and we were searching in shops for the kind of look she was after. In one shop, the security guard advised us not to go outside because there were several Jeeps parked across the street with press inside them and telephoto lenses poking out of the windows.

She didn't seem at all bothered by this and so we went out. It's the first and only time I've ever been chased up the street by the paparazzi and it was genuinely scary. She seemed completely unfazed by it – "Yeah, that's fine - just let them get the photos they want and then they'll go" – but I was quite irate.

It was made even worse by the fact that when we both got in the car, I managed to stall it. I'm just not cut out for that sort of thing.

Of shoes and bad behaviour

One of the most embarrassing situations I've ever faced involved a couple where the guy was clearly going out of his way to make the experience of selecting a ring a romantic and memorable one, and one of the really lovely things about what I do for a living is that I have a chance to get to know people a little bit and they get to know me.

In fact, the opportunity to get to know them and understand them is really important to me in developing a feel for what might interest them. So, this man had been in a couple of times and he was telling me about her and the things she likes and doesn't like, and I've got this image of a lovely girl in my head.

Eventually he decided he was going to come in with her to choose the ring.

We'd already had a conversation about his budget. We'd looked at the stones we thought she'd be interested in and those were the ones I brought out when she arrived, so he and I knew that whatever she chose from that selection would be within that budget.

None of the stones had prices on display and she went through them and, without knowing the cost of them, picked out the one she wanted.

Well, that was where it all went suddenly and badly wrong, because as a joke he turned to her and said, "Ah, you would pick the most expensive one, wouldn't you?"

And there was a deathly pause before she replied, with great indignation: "Are you serious? Does that mean I'm not getting the Christian Louboutin shoes you promised me on the way down here?"

And he went red. And I went red. And I just didn't know where to put myself. It was truly the most cringeworthy moment I've ever had in my shop. I spoke to him the following day and asked him how the shoe shopping had gone, and he was very apologetic and embarrassed about it – before telling me they'd stopped at Harrods on the way back and picked out a pair of shoes.

Things like that always feel to me like a sign of things to come. I have no idea whether they're still married – but I haven't been asked to buy back the engagement ring! If the ground could have swallowed us up, I think we'd have both been quite pleased.

A case of mistaken identical identity

I can count on the fingers of one hand – and wouldn't need all the fingers on that hand even then – the number of times I've made something and she hasn't liked it, but one of the very few occasions I did stands out in the memory.

The couple were friends of my sister and she'd suggested they come along and see me to talk about an engagement ring. So, they arrived one evening and had brought along photos of an engagement they'd seen in a shop window in Hatton Garden which she loved. They'd even gone in to the shop in question and tried on the ring.

The photos had been taken from all sorts of different angles so I could have something to work with and the name of the shop was on the label of the ring, so I knew where it was. As it happened, I knew the owner well (it's a very small world around here, as you might imagine) and so I went over and had a look and found that the pictures they'd taken were a very good representation of the ring itself.

I asked the owner where he'd got the setting from and then went and got exactly the same setting for the ring I was making for them. When it was ready, they both turned up to collect it and, as I always do, I gave it to him quietly so he could present it to her, which I think is the most appropriate way to go about things.

He was looking at it and seemed really pleased with it, saying it was spot on, perfect. Then he presented it to her and she took one look and said: "That's nothing like the ring we saw!"

I'm like, "You're joking." *He's* like, "You're joking." And she's like, "No, it's not even close." We've taken the photos out and compared them and the dispute goes on for about 20 minutes. I'm thinking to myself: *we've got pictures, we've got everything. It's the same supplier and I know it's her mind's eye playing tricks on her and convincing her it's a different thing altogether.*

He did take the ring from me and paid for it, but I learned from my sister some weeks later that they ended up going back to the other shop and he bought the ring they'd seen in the window so she had proof it was the same ring. So, he ended up with two rings.

If nothing else, it's one to tell the kids and grandchildren.

It's not all about putting a ring on her finger

Although the vast majority of the jewellery I make relates to engagement and wedding rings, or remodelling old pieces of jewellery – often old-fashioned pieces that have been inherited and the new owner wants something more contemporary – I do get the occasional request that strays from what we might call the 'norm'.

One of the stranger requests I've had was to make his and hers genital piercings in platinum with diamonds which the couple in question wanted to use to perform – by which, I might quickly add, I mean say – their vows.

I'll also add that I didn't offer a fitting service.

Do as i say, not as i do

I'm always amazed by the different ways people choose to plan the moment when they pop the question and I'm happy to give advice where I can to guys who aren't sure of the best way to present the ring. But it turns out I'm better at handing out my own advice than I am at taking it.

I got married for the second time recently and although we'd talked about getting engaged, there wasn't really a plan and my wife (as she now is) didn't know when or how it would happen.

I decided to propose whilst we were on a trip to Israel with my children. We had been together for a long time and I knew my children adored her, so I also knew there were no problems with someone new suddenly sharing their lives. The night before I was going to pop the question, as I was saying goodnight to the kids, I let them in on the secret.

I didn't get quite the reaction I was hoping for. The smiles and giggles that had preceded my big news suddenly turned to tears. They didn't want a new mummy. I spent an hour consoling them and eventually they understood that it wasn't about someone trying to be their mum, but just another adult they liked being around all the time.

With that sorted out, it looked like plain sailing until the moment came.

Except it didn't quite happen like that.

The following day, the kids stayed at home and Mandy and I went out for a walk to a little park near to my sister's apartment. We were having a chat and then I just turned to her, went down on one knee and proposed to her.

It was as my knee hit the ground that I realised we were in a dog-walking park and I'd just put my left knee in a load of dog mess. When we got back to the apartment, the first greeting I got was from my sister's dog, which came running up like I was the most important person in its world. Which I might well have been, because I probably had part of his best mate all over my trousers.

Is She Or Isn't She The One?

Like I said, it's great to get to know the couples I'm working for – because although it might just be the guy who comes in to see me on his own, I'm really working for her as well. What that also means is that the likelihood is I'll get to meet the lady after the proposal, because the chances are the ring will need to be altered.

One day a girl came in with the engagement ring I'd made for her. I'd spent a lot of time with her fiancé, working out what she would want, and I felt like I knew her, as well. As we were talking, she was really complimentary about the ring, telling me that it was probably the ring she would have chosen for herself, and as you can imagine, I was quite pleased.

By way of conversation, I asked her how he proposed.

She said: "I ruined it." This obviously wasn't the answer I was expecting, so I asked her what she meant.

It turned out that one day, she was looking for some stationery and went to look in the stationery drawer the two of them had at home. As she was going through it, she found the engagement ring hidden there.

She told me: "I thought, 'Shit, is this for me, or isn't it? And how long has it been there?'"

She didn't know what to do and so she said nothing that night, nor the night after. But she couldn't sleep properly, and she was beside herself. By the time it got to day three, she couldn't take it anymore and she just came clean and told him she'd needed stationery from the drawer and had come across the ring.

"His face dropped," she said. Luckily for both of them, it was an expression of disappointment rather than guilt. But as she pointed out, in effect she actually proposed to herself!

You'd be amazed at what's in my trunks

Many of the rings I've made have travelled round the world to get to the destination where they're presented in a proposal.

Perhaps one of the most romantic was a guy who'd spent a considerable amount of money on the ring and planned to propose on Bali. They'd flown out and were having this amazingly romantic holiday and one day he suggested the two of them snorkel out around some atolls and reefs a little way offshore.

Out they went, masks, snorkels, swimwear and as they're swimming around he just pulls this ring out from his trunks and presents it to her. They're in one of the most romantic and idyllic spots on earth and all he's wearing are the trunks. That's what got me – the fact that he was only wearing trunks and he'd secreted this really expensive engagement ring somewhere in there and then swum half a kilometre to propose.

It brings me out in a cold sweat just thinking about the ring tumbling out of his trunks – or even out of his hand as he was getting it out (no sniggering at the back) – and getting lost in the coral or on the seabed.

But that's love for you. People will go to crazy lengths to declare that their girlfriend or boyfriend is the one for them forever.

One of the nicest things about it, though, is that I do get lots of invitations to the weddings and I take up the ones that I can, because in the end, that's what I came into this business for: to make things that bring joy to people.

I wouldn't change it for anything.

IN THE PRESS

To read more about Lewis's press coverage visit www.lewismalka.com/press

THE
HUFFINGTON
POST

TESTIMONIALS

Lewis is amazing! I have known him for years! No other jeweller I would go to! Thank you for such an easy transaction with my diamond ring.
Ashly Rae

My fiancé could not have chosen better! My wonderful engagement ring, designed by Lewis Malka, is everything I could wish for. A stunning piece of art!
Monika Gierszewska

What can I say. Lewis is without question the best! He made my beautiful engagement ring which I treasure each day and one day shall pass down to my daughter. And all whilst I am living in Cornwall and Lewis in London...the distance was not an issue! Lewis makes the whole designing process exciting and all the while knowing you can trust him to make exactly what you've asked for. Lewis is the only jeweller everyone need ever know. Diamond's and Lewis are a girls best friend!
Nellie Lowe

Oh my goodness the most talented, honest brilliant Jeweller. Lewis Malka you have blown my mind. You have transformed my grandma's very old fashioned earnings and ring into a fine masterpiece. Everyone had told me for so long to use you and naturally I was sad to change the setting but I knew I would never wear it as it was. Your sensitivity was overwhelming and I love the two pieces that you clearly put your heart and soul into. Lewis - massive thank you for everything. You are one in a million and expert in your field.
Roberta Brown

Lewis helped my family with some old family jewellery. He was professional, extremely friendly and understanding given the precious nature of the items for us. I would have no hesitation to recommending Lewis to others. He has been outstanding.
Peter Gourri

The best Diamond man in Town! I have been doing business with Lewis Malka for many years. I would recommend him and never go anywhere else.
Tracy Perkins

Even though Lewis is my brother and even though I may seem a bit biased, I can't recommend him highly enough. He made my engagement and wedding rings, as well as countless repairs and other pieces over the years. You won't find a jeweller with more knowledge and passion than Lewis. He may be my brother but he's your man!
Helen Zeff

Lewis is a master craftsman - he started learning how to make jewellery at a very young age, and learned PROPERLY so he manages to still be very young AND talented at the same time. He has a wealth of knowledge about jewellery and gemstones, so can be counted on to write/speak on the topic at the drop of a hat. He is charming, personable, fun, and he really understands women - he brings this insight and empathy into his work making gorgeous jewellery and engagement rings to the super high standard. Highly recommended!
Keren Lerner

Amazing craftsmanship!!! He took all I said and made it into a perfect reality!!!!! I love my engagement ring and can't wait to get my wedding band!
Sophie Felberg

Lewis Malka designs and produces the most amazing bespoke jewellery using excellent craftsmanship and the highest quality diamonds! A genuine gent offering a truly personal service. Highly recommended.
Kelly Lynch

Amazing service, beautiful engagement ring & very happy customers! Would highly recommend Lewis.
Suzanne Hughes

Lewis is superhuman. He just gets it and understands the small details which are match winners at the end of the day. Replies to you within minutes & never says no. Would definitely recommend Lewis without any doubt whatsoever.
Gareth Edwards

I can't recommend Lewis highly enough. Fantastic service, incredibly knowledgeable and no pressure to spend more. We have worked with Lewis for engagement and wedding rings, diamond earrings, valuations, re-plating, restoration and also general advice. We have been nothing but impressed with his service.

Lauren Watkins

A Friend recommended Lewis Malka to me and I wasn't let down at all. Lewis is very relaxed and friendly. He made the very difficult decision of picking the right engagement ring easy. Carefully picking through all the styles and diamond choices. We recently returned to Lewis to get our wedding rings. Impressive selections of rings were on offer. Again the service was first class. I can't recommend Lewis Malka enough. Thanks Lewis.

Aidan O'Sullivan

Lewis made me a wedding ring for my future wife and I couldn't be happier with it. It's exactly what we were looking for and he delivered it within 3 weeks of agreeing the design. I'd have no hesitation in recommending his services.

Jonathan Snow

Lewis made me my perfect engagement ring- he knew exactly what I wanted even when I couldn't articulate it! 4 years on and I recently damaged it... Not only did I receive a very warm welcome, he fixed it up beautifully. Fantastic client service. We found Lewis by recommendation and have since recommended him to others. Not a month passes that I don't get a comment about my beautiful ring. Thanks Lewis for giving me a ring I love as much today as I did 4 years ago.

Clare John

Big thank you to Lewis who created my dream engagement ring.

Mel Pecheur

Superb service, very trustworthy, great price on a quality piece.

Jason Bird

Lewis made an absolutely gorgeous pendant for me – love, love love!!! Highly recommended - thanks again Lewis.

Jenn Read

Lewis was a gent, he saw me with little to no notice, provided me with a lovely diamond and the shank I requested all within a limited time frame and for a very reasonable price. Thanks so much Lewis the missus loves it. Keep up the good work.

Lee Ryan

Love love love my engagement ring and wedding band, so thrilled with them. Thank you so much!!

Tania Holt

I love the eternity ring you made for me - it was just what I wanted just perfect – Thank You ! It hasn't left my finger yet!!

Chev Zaitschek

Lewis Malka carried out a valuation on some inherited antique family jewellery. Thanks Lewis for the great work and the friendly service.

Lucy Campbell

I'd like to thank Lewis publicly for his excellent service. Choosing jewellery for my girlfriend seemed daunting until Lewis sat me down to answer all my questions and then some! He looked after the design, creation and delivery of the piece with typical exuberance and capability. If his professional expertise and personal flair aren't enough to sway you, his pricing surely will and that's why I'd wholeheartedly recommend his service. Thanks Lewis.

Jamie Earl

Lewis made my wife's engagement and our wedding rings. He took the time to listen and was able to deliver with the budget I provided. Since then Lewis is the only jeweller I go to and recommend. Thank you, we will be back!

Neil Zeff

Not only does Lewis make the most exquisite jewellery but he is the nicest, kindest, most high-integrity businessman I have ever had the pleasure of meeting!

Zoe Clews

THE ENGAGEMENT RING

Wish I could load a before and after picture of my ring. Went in to see Lewis to get my original engagement ring resized and walked out with two new rings. His work is spectacular, his service is impeccable and I could not be happier with the outcome. Recommended a hundred times over.

Savannah Asiza Johnston

A truly wonderful jeweller. Lewis designed and made my stunning engagement ring and then when I saw how perfect it was, I asked him to create my unique wedding ring too. His attention to detail is incredible; I was not disappointed. I would not consider going anywhere else.

Toria Bacon

Lewis Malka is absolutely the person to go to when it comes to Diamonds & Jewellery! Having known him by working in Hatton Garden, I wouldn't have gone to anyone else to get my engagement ring and subsequently wedding rings made. He is a truly great bloke, will give honest advice and knows what he is talking about. I am so pleased with his designs for both rings that I smile each time I look at them. He will, without doubt, do any future jewellery work that I may need!

Deb Garland

After having my engagement ring made and remade several times by someone else we finally went to Lewis who understood EXACTLY what I wanted and made the perfect engagement ring first time round. He was extremely patient and no detail was left out. Thank you so much!

Cassie Mann

Excellent service, great designs and I would recommend Lewis without reservation.

Alan Lewis

Whatever your budget, Lewis will without a doubt create the most exquisite ring possible for you. His innate style and creativity shine through in all of his creations. He is a truly talented artist who takes enormous pride in his work and is determined for every client to be blown away by what he makes for her.

Caroline Kendal

Lewis is a pleasure to work with always taking time to understand exactly what you want and going that extra mile. Personal service is at the heart of Lewis's business which makes a very special purchase worthwhile.

Taryn Hilburn

I feel very lucky to have met Lewis both for professional as for purely human reasons. He's an honest, fun, creative and lovely person to be around!

Ayelet Lerner

Gorgeous rings. I photographed them in detail! Much better to go for Lewis's rings than buying standard who knows what off the peg.

Rhowena MacCuish Dann

Lewis service is one of the best I've come across in any industry. Quick response, accommodating, patience and above all quality products at fair prices. He is a credit to his profession and have and will recommend him without hesitation. Top bloke too!

Peter Petrou

Lewis's passion and in depth knowledge comes through in his advice and beautifully crafted rings! Highly recommend that Lewis is your first port of call when making one of the most important decisions of your life- buying an engagement ring for your loved one.

Kemo Marriott

Top bloke, top networker and top notch, top class, top quality diamond jewellery. Lewis's attention to detail when designing his stunning pieces for his clients is second to none. Any success Lewis achieves will be thoroughly deserved as I'm yet to meet a nicer person in business who doesn't stop when trying to help others succeed.

Craig Lesser

I was admiring one of Lewis's extraordinary beautiful diamond rings on someone's finger just the other day, sadly not my own but he'd be the first person I'd go to for diamond jewellery! His pieces are truly stunning and his passion for diamond jewellery is evident. He's also wonderful to work with so I wouldn't hesitate in recommending his services to anyone I know.

Mel Hales

The passion Lewis has for his job shines out in absolutely everything he does. Lewis made me the most beautiful engagement ring, taking the time to listen and understand exactly what I am looking for. I have since recommended Lewis to two of my friends who have been over the moon at his personalised service and beautiful work. He literally does bring a woman to tears in the very best way possible. I highly recommend Lewis to anyone looking for that beautiful piece to be made or restored.

Carey Kolver Goate.

I've no hesitation in recommending Lewis Malka to anyone looking for advice or assistance in the diamond or jewellery world. It's a minefield and Lewis' patient and knowledgeable approach really put me at ease as soon as we met. Whether it's a beautiful unique design by him, or drawing inspiration from a designer ring you had in mind, he will always produce the highest quality piece and really offers far better value for your money than the high street or well known brands. Top diamond geezer!

Rachel Dobson

Lewis has it all! He is totally attentive to his clients, their tastes and means. His enthusiasm, knowledge and skills combine to produce top class diamond jewellery to please the most discerning client and the provide the best value.

Bernard Gunther

I have known Lewis since 2007 and have used his services both personally and professionally. He made my partner Lisa a fabulous pair of diamond stud earrings. Having carried out a bit of research on the high street as most people do, it soon became apparent I could get much more for my money using Lewis. Better diamonds, bespoke service and all delivered in a lovely professional manner. I also recommend Lewis to my clients. As Head of Private Clients at James Hallam Insurance Brokers having a jeweller I can trust to be discreet and offer exceptional service is really important. If you need a jeweller there really is no reason not to consider Lewis.

Mike Nightingale

Lewis made my beautiful engagement ring earlier this year. I didn't know what I wanted and he guided me expertly through the options and suggested what might suit me. I couldn't be happier. There isn't a day goes by without someone commenting on how sparkly and beautiful it is. My fiancé and I are over the moon with it. Thank you Lewis.

Josephine Watterson

Lewis made my engagement and wedding ring, as well as other jewellery for me over the years. I have been delighted with his professional and knowledgeable approach and have no hesitation in recommending Lewis to all my family and friends. Thank you Lewis. See you again very soon!

Katie Kibel

Friendly and professional, that's Lewis Malka! He knows everything and anything you need to know about diamonds. Definitely staying in the phone book as the go-to-diamond-guy.

Khara Sawyer

ENGAGEMENT RING GALLERY

TRADITIONAL FOUR-WIRE SETTING

FOUR-CLAW CROSS WIRE SETTING

PARALLEL TWIST STYLE DESIGN

CLASSIC SIX-CLAW OPEN SET DESIGN

TRADITIONAL SIX-WIRE SET DESIGN

TRADITIONAL CORONET SETTING

ENGAGEMENT RING GALLERY

SINGLE ROW HALO STYLE

SOLITAIRE WITH BAGUETTE STYLE SHOULDERS

FOUR-CLAW OPEN SET RING

SOLITAIRE WITH CHANNEL-SET SHOULDERS

SOLITAIRE WITH PAVE SHOULDERS

ART DECO STYLE RING

THE ENGAGEMENT RING

INSTAGRAM GALLERY

INSTAGRAM GALLERY

THE ENGAGEMENT RING

RING SIZE CHART
(AVERAGE SIZES)

UK	US	Italy	Europe	Inside Diameter
J	4 ¾	5.5	49	14.48mm
J ½	5	6	49.5	15.67mm
K	5 ¼	10	50	15.87mm
K ½	5.5	10.5	50.5	16.06mm
L	5 ¾	11/11.5	51	16.26mm
L ½	6	11.5/12	52	16.45mm
M	6 ¼	12/12.5	53	16.65mm
M ½	6.5	13	53.5	16.84mm
N	6 ¾	13.5	54	17.04mm
N ½	7	14/14.5	54.5	17.24mm
O	7 ¼	15	55	17.45mm
O ½	7.5	15.5	55.5	17.65mm
P	7 ¾	16	56	17.86mm
P ½	8	16.5	57	18.06mm
Q	8 ¼	17	58	18.27mm
Q ½	8.5	18/18.5	58.5	18.47mm
R	8 ¾	19	59	18.68mm
R ½	9	19.5	60	18.88mm
S	9 ¼	20	60.5	19.09mm
S ½ - T	9.5	21	61	19.41mm

Lightning Source UK Ltd.
Milton Keynes UK
UKHW052017170622
404585UK00006B/263